The Dra~~~ ~~ ~~~~~
and other judo stories
in the Zen tradition

THE
DRAGON
MASK

AND OTHER
JUDO STORIES
IN THE ZEN
TRADITION

trevor
LEGGETT

Published by
Ippon Books Ltd.
HR House,
447 High Road,
Finchley, London
N12 0AF UK

British Library Cataloguing in Publication Data
Leggett, Trevor
The Dragon Mask
and other judo stories in the Zen tradition

ISBN 1874572 16 X

Design: Miles Holt
Printed by Redwood Books, Trowbridge, Wiltshire.

Acknowledgments

Ippon Books acknowledges the use of stories
which originally appeared in Budo; Zen and
the Ways (Routledge and Kegan Paul);
A First Zen Reader (Tuttle) ; and in talks
given to The Buddhist Society, London
(collated by Ben Andersen);
and to The Budokwai,
(Frank Ward recording 1993).

Picture credits:
Illustrations selected by Ippon Books Ltd.with thanks to the British
Museum, London (P. 10, P.109). Camera Press (P.119). Judo
sequence demonstrated by Kisaburo Watanabe, courtesy of Tuttle
(P.54). (P.60) Hugh O'Donnell. (P.115) Takamasu Imamura.

Trevor Leggett

Trevor Pryce Leggett was born in London in 1914. He graduated from the University of London (L.L.B) in 1934. In 1939 he went to Japan and on the outbreak of war in Europe joined the British Embassy in Tokyo, where he served until 1942. After World War II, he joined the BBC; he headed the Japanese service of the BBC from 1946 to 1970.

Since his retirement from the BBC, he has appeared on many of its Japanese programmes and at the same time has published books and articles on various cultural aspects of both Britain and Japan. For his contribution to introducing Japanese culture to Britain, he was awarded the Order of the Sacred Treasure by the Japanese government in 1984.

T.P. Leggett began judo in 1930 at The Budokwai, London, at the age of 16, taught by Yukio Tani, 4th Dan, and Gunji Koizumi, 4th Dan. He took part in international competitions and, by the time he arrived in Japan in 1939, was 3rd Dan.

On his return to the UK after the war, he resumed his judo practice at The Budokwai where he was senior instructor (1954-1964) and a major influence in the rising generation of British judoka, encouraging both a high level of technical study and a broader cultural interest.

He holds 9th Dan from the British Judo Association and 6th Dan from the Kodokan. An enthusiastic shogi player, he has 5th Dan from the Japan Shogi Federation.

He has written some thirty books. Among them are: Zen and the Ways; The First Zen Reader; Championship Judo – Tai-Otoshi and Ouch-Gari Attacks; Cloth and Stone – Stories of Yoga and Zen and The Spirit of Budo.

Table of Contents

Judo and the ways 10
Introduction 13
Outer and inner balance 19
Judo and shuji 23
The cherry tree 27
Question 31
Efficiency of the heart 34
Specialisation 39
Help 43
Limits of technique 44
Humble 47
Dr Kano's washing 49
Ingenuity 50
The tradition of judo 54
Judo koan 55
Beginners 58
Kind-hearted 60
Hard and soft 63
Irrelevances 65
Ippon-yari 67
Run-up 69
Sacrifices 71
Special duties 72
Excuses 75
The dragon mask I 76

The dragon mask II 80
Onshi 83
Tricks 89
Manners 92
The killer instinct 93
A lovely style 94
Cutting off the 95
  bull's horns
Tigers and Rabbits 97
Specialities 98
Predicting the result 100
The new black belt 102
Inspiration 104
Kangeiko 106
Disadvantages 107
The learning process 112
Surprise 113
Falling 114
Faith 116
Endurance 118
Quick 119
Even effort 122
Hold 127

Judo and the ways

Since its inclusion on the Olympic programme in 1964, judo has become so much part of the international sports programme that it is only too easy to forget that it had its origins in a very different tradition – the honoured Japanese tradition of Do or The Way.

When Jigoro Kano reformulated his system from its ju-jitsu forbears, he took great care in deciding upon a name. His choice of Judo – The Gentle (or Yielding) Way – signified, for Kano and his contemporaries, the nature of the activity itself.

The Ways have a long history in Japan, though they were particularly developed during the Edo period – from the 16th century. The concept was simple yet profound: through the rigorous and lively practice of an art, a mature character could emerge.

The actual form or art was not so important – the very variety in Japanese culture reflects the range of human interest and human nature. Among them are *bushido* (the way of the warrior), *chado* (the way of tea), *kyudo* (the way of the bow), *shodo* (the way of the brush) and *kendo* (the way of the sword).

Judo is part of this tradition. However, Trevor Leggett mentions that judo is a difficult Way to follow because it is so complex technically and it is only too easy to become enmeshed in the pure mechanics of it all. On the other hand, it can be an effective medium of changing and developing the personality because it does not involve any external tool – there is no brush, no spear, no bowl of tea, or bow. There is just us.

In this invigorating collection, Leggett gives memorable pointers to the use of judo as a Way. There is always a danger with fashionable Zen stories that they become mere diverting entertainments. But the merit of **The Dragon Mask and other judo stories in the Zen tradition** is that no one who has met Trevor Leggett, or had the benefit of studying under him, can doubt that these stories come from the heart – and that they have been put into practice before finding their way onto the page.

Therefore, however entertaining they may be, it is best not to read many at a sitting, but absorb them gradually over a period. That, in itself, may be a little lesson...

Nicolas Soames
Ippon Books

Bamboo in moonlight. Ink painting on silk.

Introduction

Judo is not football.
When we are young, we play football, and we are told, 'Try and win, try and win'. But the main purpose is to develop our physique. It's not for most schoolboys to become professional footballers.

In the same way, judo is to give you something for life, and for most of us it is not to become contest leaders.

Dr Jigoro Kano, the founder of judo, regarded judo as a training for life. He thought it was much better for this than ball games which are not natural activities.

But fighting is a natural activity and if the natural activity can be spiritualised and made rational, so that instead of making enemies, you are making friends, then it will give you something for life.

Imagination and Open Judo
But it is much more than that. In order to safeguard the health of competitors, contest judo has become narrower and narrower. The rules have been narrowed down and every time they are narrowed, the opportunities for the small man are limited. And that means there's a poverty of imagination.

I suggest you should go back and introduce in your *randori* – which, after all, means **free practice** – open judo, in which everything is allowed except striking. Allow people to hold the belt; allow people to hold the sleeve.

Don't rely on winning as the sole objective but developing skill. This will help us in life.

I am a big man and I was fairly strong, but I must admit against a short chap when he caught the end of the belt my heart used to sink

– because he could whirl in and put the belt over his shoulder and over I would go. Here, he was using his imagination.

Let your randori partners hold the end of the belt or the trouser leg – anything to get the man over. Then, imagination will develop and it will be an advantage for life.

So I would suggest that you bring in open judo and keep the contest rules narrow.

The idea was to develop energy for life and courage for life. I have compared notes with people who have been through similar experiences and most of us have said that a judo contest is just as bad a strain on the nerves as real danger of life and death. It is a very good training for that.

Judo must train the imagination. Work out your own methods and have open judo practise. Not concentrating on 'you are not going to beat me'. In that way, both sides will benefit. This was one of Dr Kano's main principles, that both sides will benefit in this antagonistic activity.

Weaknesses

Through judo training, we learn our bodies have limitations. We are weak in certain respects. These have to be corrected to some extent.

The Japanese say that every man has seven big faults of character. In judo we learn how to minimise our faults and how to develop beyond them. We must not try and avoid the faults, but cultivate a proper method of dealing with them. For instance, if I am right-handed and I am left to my own devices, I will simply use the right hand more and more. But a good teacher will make me use the left side, and then the co-ordination of the whole body will be improved about the centre line.

So it is to bring to life the left side which is relatively neglected. Judo should help us to do that, not only on the mat but in life.

Stances

'Oh no, I've never been any good with figures.'
'I can't understand these legal things.'

'I don't get on with people.'

'I get on with people all right, but where I am no good is when I am on my own.'

All these are weaknesses, and judo should help us to confront those weaknesses with courage and go for them.

A Japanese chess champion I knew could sit in front of the board for 10 minutes, a quarter of an hour, half an hour without moving a muscle and without making a move.

His opponent was fidgeting, going to the lavatory, having a drink, lighting cigarettes.

The old boy just sat there.

After he had won, I talked to him and he wasn't at all this calm figure, but a wisecracking Tokyo cockney. I asked, 'How is it that your chess personality is so different to your ordinary personality?'

He said, 'Well, when I was young I was like that young chap, impatient, fidgety, and I realised that I would always lose to an old boy who can just sit there. So I practised sitting in front of an empty board for an hour every day for a week, then two hours every day for a week without moving.'

'Now I can outsit the best of them.'

This is the sort of thing which judo should help us to do – to confront our weak points.

Training

We have training. Judo teaches us training. You have to train, but you have to be spontaneous. If you start being spontaneous without training, your bad habits will get worse and worse.

If you are one-sided, you won't naturally develop into two-sided. You will become more one-sided.

When you see somebody who can't type, they start with two fingers. If they go on typing like that, they won't gradually use ten fingers. They will get better and better at using this terrible method. The hands move very fast like a couple of mad hens. But they never develop a good technique and the result is that typing is always a strain and an effort.

Now the purpose of judo technique is to show you this and enable you to master what has been learnt in the past – and then to become spontaneous and free.

You have to train and then you have to jump beyond the training.

Spontaneity
When the time comes, we have to jump.

We should learn the right technique, but there is something else that judo can give us if we really train.

We have our *tokui waza* – this is how I am going to win. We rely on it. But the psychological training is to go in and forget all your favourite things and just throw yourself in totally. It is very difficult to do. But if you succeed in doing it, something new will come. The body seems to move by itself. And quite often it is something that you are not very expert at.

This is one of the things which the old masters stressed. That the Way comes to an end. You train and train and now you have got to forget that training and open yourself. This applies to life.

We have got our pet techniques in life.

'I always look at things scientifically.'

'Well you have got to be a bit practical, you know.'

'Well, what about the feelings of other people?'

We keep on repeating our favourite lines.

'I'm the one who is always thinking of other people. I am the conscience of other people.'

'I am the one who has got cool objective scientific viewpoints.'

'I am the one who says get on with life.'

We have got these favourite tricks which we use in life and we have got to be able to jump beyond them.

The blind spot
And if you can, what happens?

This is called the blind spot. It is something that is well known but is rarely thought about or analysed.

The chemist, Linus Pauling, who was continuously creative over a number of years, said, 'When I am confronted with a problem that defeats me, I concentrate on it for three weeks. Then I deliberately rely on my subconscious and throw away all thought of it. And then weeks, or months, and sometimes years later, the answer suddenly pops into my mind.'

Now, we have no explanation for these things. None. The great French mathematician Poincaré tried to analyse it. He said, ' It means that there is something in my unconscious mind that is more intelligent than I am! It can solve problems which I can't solve. I would hate to think that!'

We are given the chance in judo – there is a tradition – to practise emptying the mind. After the judo practise, when you are pouring with sweat and blood you practise sitting still.

We used to do this at the black belt classes which we held at The Budokwai. It is said to give energy, an inspiration and a freedom. It can even give freedom from the fear of death.

To be able to empty the mind, like a clear space. Not falling asleep. Like a clear space, empty of hopes, ambitions, fears, and worries.

This is the advantage of learning an art like judo. In a small field, you can practise this emptying the mind and you will receive inspiration. Something will happen which you don't direct. The body will move of itself. It will come to life.

Bushi of the Yin, Bushi of the Yang
One of the old texts say there are two kinds of *bushi* (the Japanese warriors) – the *bushi* of the *yin* (the quiet) and the *bushi* of the *yang* (the positive).

The *bushi* of the *yang*, the positive, walks as if his feet would crush the earth. His glare looks as if it would powder rocks. He walks on with small steps uttering shouts which terrify the opponents.

The *bushi* of the *yin* is calm. He walks steadily. He is silent. But the response is instant because he is not making the response – the response is coming from the beyond.

These are some of the traditions within judo. And in judo we can try them. This is one of the things judo can give us for life: energy, courage – but also the ability in difficulties, or in triumph and success, to be free from it all.

> *O-me-dame de shinde koi.*
> With wide open eyes come and die.

This dying means give up the thoughts on which we rely. Give up the things we hold on to and walk forward with wide open eyes.

These are some of the things that judo is meant to give us – and can give us if we practise in that way.

It is not wrong to practise in other ways. But we ought to think, occasionally, if it can give us more than just fighting on the mat.

Outer and inner balance

People who live in towns (in other words, most people) keep themselves upright by looking at the walls when they are indoors, and looking at the corners of the buildings when they are outside. They use these things to tell them what is vertical. This is proved by putting people in special rooms where the walls are slightly tilted to one side. When they are asked to walk across such a room, they walk unsteadily. They must continually adjust their balance. However much they try, they unconsciously align themselves with the walls, which means that they tend to lean a little to one side.

If they are told to shut their eyes, they can walk fairly steadily. But with shut eyes, an ordinary person cannot balance himself very well, because his inner balance is weak. A footballer or skater put in the room does much better: he is trained to feel his balance internally; he does not rely much on outside verticals to keep upright. After all, there are no outside vertical lines on a football ground or a skating rink. But even he may become unsteady occasionally; when he is indoors, he may have developed a habit of relying on the straight walls.

The trained judo man does best of all. He never relies on outside things, but has his whole feeling of balance inside him. He can stand up well in a high wind, because he is used to being pushed strongly.

The principle of developing inner balance should extend far beyond the judo hall. In life, most people judge what to do by looking at outside standards; often they simply do what other people are doing. They have no inner standards. But we should train in life as we train physically on the judo *tatami* (mat). We must learn to meet the shocks and changes of life flexibly, without losing inner balance.

Suppose there is something which upsets us. If we practise controlling our immediate reaction we shall find that after one or two years we no longer respond involuntarily to that situation.

There are various methods of practising control: a traditional *budo* (martial arts) one is to pause before doing anything and take several deep slow breaths, centering the attention on the navel. After that little break, make the response to the situation. The response will not now be based on some instinct like anger or fear, but will be controlled and appropriate. It is called in the *budo* books 'having a little margin in life.'

It is perhaps a bit similar to the idea of what is called 'tolerance' in machinery. When there are two parts of a machine which have to slide against each other, they must not be too tight. There should be a small space between them, so that they can slide easily. If there is no space, and the metals are pressed tightly against each other, they will generate heat and friction, and quickly wear each other out. In the same way in life, when people have to get along with each other, there should be just a small space between them. Then they can move easily and things go well. But if they are too tightly pressed against each other, tightly bound together by ties of liking or disliking, then heat will develop, and ultimately friction, and finally they will wear each other out.

Someone who has trained in this way begins to get an inner balance in life. He is not upset when outer supports and friends leave him; he does not stagger, relying on false outer standards.

This does not mean furiously refusing to do something just because everyone else is doing it. That can be a blind rebelliousness, just as false as the standards which it is supposed to be rejecting. The proper training gives inner calm, which can see clearly what is the effective action in the situation that comes up.

To live with a little margin gives balance. The principle can even be a help to other people. I remember a rather exceptional case when I was head of the Japanese Service of the British Broadcasting Corporation. Occasionally guest speakers are invited to broadcast, and usually they manage fairly well. The audience does not expect that a guest speaker will be as expert as the professional broadcasters on the staff. But before inviting someone to broadcast, one has to judge what he or she will be able to do. There are people who become very nervous when facing a microphone for the first time, and realise that very many people will be listening to them (we used to get 250,000 letters every year from Japanese listeners).

It can happen, however, that someone who is confident beforehand suddenly becomes nervous when they see the studio. On this occasion it happened. He was the head of a Japanese trade mission, and he was to read a short statement, telling the Japanese public what they had achieved. He seemed quite at ease until we came to the studio for the rehearsal. Then he suddenly became very nervous. He read over his statement, but he kept making mistakes, or missing out a word, and things like that. Then he did not know what to do: whether to begin the sentence again, or just to go on as if nothing had happened. Each time he was getting worse.

The Japanese staff member who was coaching him began to look very anxious. I was watching from the control cubicle, and had a sudden idea. I went in to the studio and sat down opposite the guest. I told him: 'I do not want you to worry about mistakes. Your mission has been a big success, and it is not good if you just read your statement correctly in an even voice. It would not sound natural. If you find you are doing that, please deliberately make one or two mistakes. Then it will sound much more natural. Some of our most famous broadcasters make a point of putting in little occasional hesitations or mistakes, just to make it more lively.'

He looked at me, and relief spread all over his face. All the tenseness dropped away. As a matter of fact, he read it perfectly, and only remembered to put in a little hesitation right at the end. He had been given a margin, and that had restored his balance.

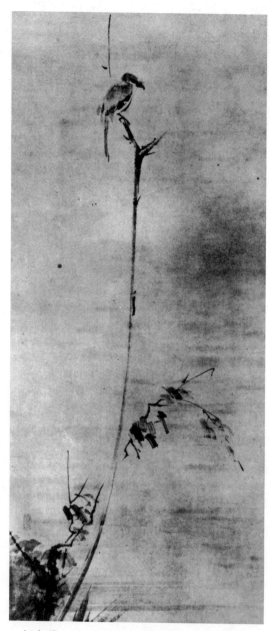

A shrike on a twig by Miyamoto Musashi.

Judo and shuji

When I had been a few months in Japan and had learnt a few hundred of the most frequently occurring Chinese characters, and became able to read a sentence here and there which was written in those common characters, I felt quite pleased with my progress. But then I found that for anything beyond simple sentences, one would need to know not a couple of hundred more, but a couple of thousand more.

I set to work, but began to get bored with the drudgery of it. Like most foreigners at this stage, I experienced a sort of oceanic weariness. Each new character had to be written out twenty times in order to learn it, but for each hundred new characters one learnt, it seemed that one forgot some old ones. 'You cram them into your head in the day,' complained one student, 'but you find that in the night they have leaked away out of your heels.' One seemed to be swimming through a sea of weird shapes without any glimpse of a far shore.

Many of us gave up. I was determined to go on, but looked about for something that would lighten the task, or at least make it more interesting. Finally I got the idea of studying *shuji* (calligraphy). I heard that one of the Embassy teachers was an expert, and took a weekly lesson with him.

He quickly understood that I was taking up calligraphy to help myself to learn the characters, and he co-operated very well. He told me many interesting and unusual mnemonics: *uri wa tsume ari; tsume wa tsume nashi* – the Chinese character for Claw has no claw; the character for Melon is very like it but has a claw. After 55 years I still remember this, and many other such, which shows how effective they are in supporting memory. I also remember clearly some of the interesting methods of instruction in calligraphy.

In the Grass Hand style, the characters are written in a very abbreviated and flowing form. Some of the elements of the characters come again and again, and have the same Grass Hand form. One of them is a particular element which comes on the right side, and is generally the last big stroke of the Grass Hand. Ideally, the teacher said, this vertical stroke should have a very slight curve in it. When I was told this, I wrote it with a curve, but he always said that the curve was too pronounced. 'It must be very, very slight,' he said, and demonstrated. I could not manage it. Either I wrote it with a perfectly straight vertical stroke, or else, when I tried to make it a curve, that was said to be too much. When my efforts were put side by side with one of his, I could see what he meant, but I could not do it. I think my efforts amused him just a little.

Finally he told me: 'Write it, large, with a curve, a hundred times, till you have filled two sheets of paper.' I did this getting more and more facility with it as I wrote it again and again. Then he put a blank sheet of paper in front of me. 'Now,' he said, 'write that character with a perfectly vertical stroke – no curve at all.' I dashed it off. There was the very slight curve which I had been unable to make. When I had done it once or twice, I got the knack of it. The teacher said: 'Now forget all about straight lines and curves. It will be natural to you now.'

I found this concrete experience useful in appreciating Japanese culture. For instance, I heard this about some traditional Japanese black and white paintings. We foreigners used to expect paintings to be representational, even if they were very simple sketches. The Japanese method of painting, which seems to depend on suggestion, is strange to us.

For instance, I heard the criticism of Miyamoto Musashi's famous painting of a bird sitting alertly on a twig: 'I feel uneasy when I look at this picture. That slender twig could not support the weight of the bird. It is simply impossible. Why did he not make the twig thicker?' Again, sometimes we see a Japanese picture of a mountain, which is not Mount Fuji, reflected in a lake. But the reflection in the water has the shape of Mount Fuji.

Westerners feel uneasy when they see this. I remember hearing a Japanese trying to explain that all mountains remind Japanese of Mount Fuji, and the reflection is intended to convey that inner thought. But his little audience did not understand.

On another occasion, a foreigner at an art exhibition at Ueno said to a Japanese critic: 'I cannot understand these pictures. I want to understand them. I feel that there is some great beauty hidden in them. But I cannot do it. I keep noticing some detail which seems to me quite unreal.' The Japanese answered him: 'If you really want to understand, you can. Stand in front of a picture for ten minutes, and look at it in detail. Now continue standing and looking, but forget the ink-strokes, forget what you think it represents, forget the paper, forget the art gallery and that you are in it. When you have forgotten all that, what remains is the beauty.' The foreigner looked a bit bewildered, but he did what he had been told, and he said later that he had begun to appreciate Japanese painting.

I had a somewhat different instruction about calligraphy. After a couple of years, I could execute a reasonable copy of the *kanji* (Japanese characters) brushed by my teacher, or in the book. But I could not understand the basis of some of his criticisms. He would say: 'this one you have done well, but that one is rather lifeless.' When I looked at them, I could not see any particular difference between them. I could see that they were not exactly the same, but I could not see that one was better than the other. I said this to the teacher, and he pondered for a bit, but said nothing.

The next time he came he gave me quite a surprise. He got me to write a few *kanji* which I knew well. Then he picked out two, and put them alongside each other. 'Look at those two,' he said. I dutifully stared at them. 'You say that you do not see that one is better than the other? You cannot see that one is well balanced and full of life, and the other is sagging?' 'I don't see any special difference,' I admitted. Then he said: 'You are a judo man. Now forget about calligraphy, forget about the brush and the paper. Look at that character on the left as if it were a judo opponent. Can't you see that it is well balanced, full of spring and life? And this one on the right – if that were a judo man, what would you think of his posture? Forget the strokes, forget all you have learnt about calligraphy, forget that this is a written character: look at them as if they were living judo men on the *tatami.*' I found this a bit bewildering at first, but after a little time I did indeed begin to feel the life in one, and the lack of life in the other.

Somehow it caused a reaction in me: looking at the lively one, I felt my body becoming alert as it did when facing a judo opponent poised for attack. When I looked at the other one, I felt my body saying to me: 'Slack, he's slack. There is nothing there to worry about.' After that striking experience I became a much better judge of the written *kanji*. The teacher said some time later: 'You are getting a good feeling for the characters.'

Some years later, I read in one of the traditional *kendo* scrolls (manuals of Japanese fencing) that *kendo* could be practised mentally. 'Sit in *seiza* and go into meditation. Visualise an opponent striking at you, and your own sword meeting his, and countering. The movements should be fast but smooth, as if brushing *kanji*.' When I read this, I understood what it meant. I realised my experience had been only half of the Budo principle: I had used my judo skill to help me with the brush. But this was using visualisation of brush strokes to help with *kendo* technique, and it must also apply to judo technique.

I have never heard a judo teacher give definite instruction on these lines. But perhaps there are hints in our tradition that to practise *shuji* will help with judo.

I do not know of any comparable tradition in the Western cultures. There have been a few geniuses who have hinted at such things, but they could not pass anything on to their pupils. There was no background of tradition to support them.

In Japan, there was.

The cherry tree

The cherry tree blossoms for three weeks. For the remaining forty-nine, nothing shows above the ground, but the roots are going deeper and deeper. The phrase in the Chinese Book of Change is: 'The thunder is buried in the earth.' The vitality is in the roots. That long time of apparent inertia, and the short period of blossoming, form a unity. It is not that the cherry tree is depressed and sad, and a failure for a long time, but then has a wonderful success, which is, alas, all too passing, all too quickly taken away. No: this is a single tree, not two trees.

The human being, especially the poet, sees the moment of glory, and a long dull stretch when the life is in the roots as two things. But they are one.

In the West there is a tendency to think of a tree or plant in terms of what is above ground only, though in fact the roots are sometimes many times bigger. If we are asked to describe or draw a tree, we present the trunk and branches. But the Chinese character representing a tree shows the roots as well, much more extensive than the branches.

The same point comes up in judo. An experienced teacher looks at a number of keen young students, and notes how the build differs. They all have physical and psycho–physical habits, some good and some bad. For a time the training tends to be the same; it is concerned with all-round development of body, balance, and anticipation; much of the training is ironing out the fixed habits. Later, the teacher brings out the natural facilities of that pupil.

Now suppose that he can see that a particular pupil could excel in a certain throw, which is however rather difficult. If he considers him strong enough in persistence, he may show him the throwing action, and say: 'When you have practised this a hundred thousand times, you will get the feeling of it. There's a sort of knack of timing, which can't be imitated or taught. It can only be felt.'

But if you do the practice, you'll get it. To do a hundred thousand practice attacks with this throw is going to take some time. They must not be mere repetitions, which soon become mechanical and sloppy. They must each have a keen edge of trying for the inner feel of the throw. If he does a hundred a day, assuming a six-day week, he could do it in three years. Then it will be part of him: he will not have 'mastered the throw' but it will be as natural to him as blinking or sneezing. But it would be quite wrong for him to think, after one year of the practice, 'Oh well, of course, I have got still two years to go; I can't get it yet.' Not at all – he may get it any time. The teacher has not told him: 'You will have to do a hundred thousand before you get it.' What he told him was: 'After a hundred thousand, you will certainly have got it.' He may have got it long before that. As he begins his daily hundred, he must think: 'I'll get it now, I'm going to get it now.'

It is not just a question of faith in the teacher. The student must realise that the teacher has faith in him, the student himself. He would not teach it to him, unless he had that faith. When the pupil has faith in the teacher's faith, he will keep it up.

Failure and failure and failure – but he keeps going. Then suddenly (it is usually sudden), the throw begins to come to him. As the old teachers used to say: 'The god of *waza* (technique) comes up in him.' This may happen long before the hundred thousand figure has been reached. From the pupil's standpoint, it is like a sort of wonder, sunlight breaking through clouds. But the teacher's view is different. To him, the thousands of failures, and the final success, are not two: they are a unity. On the judo cherry tree the failures are the root, and the success is the blossom. The tree is not failing and failing, and then suddenly succeeding. The roots were going deeper all the time when there was little surface change.

A keen student must also be on the watch for what are called in judo circles by various uncomplimentary names. One of the least offensive is 'old soldiers'. One of them will say to him: 'Look. I've been here fourteen years.' (His grade is not very high, but he is quite impressive with his reminiscences of past masters.) 'You've been told to practise that a hundred thousand times, haven't you! Well, they say that to everybody – sometimes it's sixty thousand, sometimes a hundred and twenty thousand. But they don't expect anyone to actually DO it. It's impossible; no one could keep it up. And if you did keep it up, you'd simply get hopelessly stale and sick of it. No, they just tell you these things to get you to do serious training, that's all. And with your build, you'll never be any good at that particular throw. The teacher doesn't expect it. But practising it will probably improve your movement a bit, and that's what he wants. He doesn't tell you that, of course.'

When a pupil of about eighteen is told this sort of thing by some old boy who seems to have been there a long time and to have seen it all and known it all, he tends to be impressed. He's likely to think: 'Is that right? Do they just say these things to everyone without really meaning them? I wonder...'

A young teacher, when he sees what is happening, tends to get uneasy and think: 'He's being talked out of this.' He may ask an old teacher whether he should give the pupil a word of reassurance.

The old teacher says: 'No! Certainly not. Look at you. In your contest days, you were county champion, then in the national team. Then as a teacher, you have produced some first rate judo men – and you've published a couple of books (one of them was quite good) on judo. Well known, aren't you? Now that boy's either going to believe you or he's going to believe that no-good man who's never done anything himself and doesn't want anyone else to do anything either. So leave him alone. If he can't have faith in you now, he'll always have to be pushed and encouraged. And that's no basis for a judo man.'

In the West there are some other 'old soldiers'. Especially intellectual old soldiers. 'What is the use of practising', (they argue), 'until you have the throw perfect? If you practise before it is perfect, then you are practising your mistakes. So you will not get better – you will get worse.' The argument is stupid. A child learning to ride a bicycle keeps falling off – but he is not practising mistakes. He is searching for the sense of balance, and finally he gets it. Practice makes perfect: you do not have to be a perfect practiser when you begin.

The same point comes up in many inner disciplines. For instance, students of *mantra* are told by an Indian teacher that the *mantra* will awaken in them after three million attentive repetitions. Instead of getting a pocket calculator and working it out – that an hour's repetition each day would reach the total in about seven years – they simply assume it is impossible. Why then is it said? 'Well you see, this is meant for Indians. Now Indians are a very extreme people: think of those yogis on the bed of nails, or living naked in the Himalayas. Everything in India has to be set out in very extreme forms. That is what they are used to. If it was not put like that, they just wouldn't accept anything at all. But it is not meant that ordinary people are to follow the instructions literally.'

Sometimes they forget what they said before, and produce the opposite excuse: 'Well you see, Indians are very lazy people. Think of all those yogis in the Himalayas, running away from the world and doing nothing. To get Indians to do even a little bit, you have to tell them to do a tremendous lot. No one expects them actually to do it all, or even very much. It's just a way of getting SOMETHING out of them. But that doesn't apply here, of course. When they say three million, they just mean a few hundred. One has to use one's own judgement.'

Whether it is in yoga or in judo or in anything else, the people who apply their own 'judgement' to vary, and ultimately contradict, a teacher's instructions, usually end up as little discussion groups on the sidelines.

Judges need to have some qualifications.

Question

Does not competitive sport produce discord? If so, should it not be avoided by a seeker of the Way, whether as participator or even spectator?

If people play golf or soccer or chess or judo, without counting points to make a match of it, that is not sport but healthy exercise (mental in the case of chess). It may create no discord, but it is tasteless and ultimately boring.

If they count points, but are competing to make money or reputation, this is not sport but business. It does create discord among players and also often among spectators too.

The essence of sport is that two or more agree to PLAY at being enemies, on a fixed field under fixed rules. They try with intense seriousness to win. If the sides are fairly evenly matched, so that sometimes one wins and sometimes the other, there is a special zest. They have voluntarily entered a closed field of opposition where they exercise will-to-win; if luck plays some part (like gusts of wind in golf), then ingenuity is taxed also.

One of the few real pleasures in life is to adopt the role of antagonist seriously, yet knowing that there is a unity at the heart of the situation. After the match, the contestants smile at each other. Regular contests between closely matched opponents should make a strong friendship. Think of Dickens's portrait of Sarah Battle at whist.

I may add that in Zen the traditional British notion of the good sportsman, who tries very hard but yet transcends winning-and-losing, is highly esteemed. (Japanese, and many others, are often furious when they lose, and exultant when they win.) Some teachers say that life itself is a game to be played in this way: with serious efforts, and yet an underlying transcendence of life-and-death.

So true competitive sport is a temporary make-believe discord in an underlying real concord, and it is a good way of refining the instinctive drives in human nature.

Dr. Jigoro Kano, the founder of judo

Efficiency of the heart

Dr. Kano, the founding father of judo, put forward what he called the 'principle of highest efficiency' as one of the central pillars of his system. He used to give illustrations in the physical field which are familiar to all students of judo; for instance, unnecessary force should not be used in making a throw, but just enough to make it succeed. This was contrary to some of the older *jujitsu* teachings that the whole of the body-force should be put into the throw. Dr. Kano gave some illustrations from the field of ordinary behaviour.

I remember when I heard him speak about argument and debate. I was then about seventeen years old, and very energetic. I sometimes used to get excited in an argument, and begin to shout. As I was big and even then fairly strong, sometimes my opponent would become nervous, and would stop arguing against me. So I found this quite a good method of winning an argument. At least, I thought it was a good method. But Dr. Kano in his lecture said something like this: 'In an argument, you may silence an opponent by pressing an advantage of strength, or of wealth, or of education. But you do not really convince him. Though he is no longer saying anything, in his heart he still keeps his opinion. The only way to make him change that opinion is to speak quietly and reasonably. When he understands that you are not trying to defeat him, but only to find the truth, he will listen to you and perhaps accept what you tell him.'

This was quite a surprise to me. But these words, spoken in beautiful English by this cultured Japanese gentleman, had a big effect: my behaviour began to change. I realised that my attitude to an argument had been inefficient, because it had brought in something quite unnecessary: namely a desire to win. To bring in such things is against the principle of highest efficiency. Dr. Kano had recommended us to study the application of this principle everywhere in life, and my interest in it was now roused. I did indeed discover it as a sort of efficiency of the heart and mind, and found it in very unexpected places. I will give a few examples. These were things which I had half noticed, but never understood. The first two examples are typing, and shorthand.

Before I went to London University, I thought it would be a good idea to master these two skills. At that time, very few students thought like this. But in fact, they gave me a great advantage. I was studying law. Some lecturers spoke slowly, and students could write most of what they said down in their ordinary handwriting. They were dealing with parts of law where the main thing was to memorise. We students took down the lectures, read some of the books, and learnt much of it by heart. But there are other parts of law where students have to be trained to think. These lecturers spoke rather quickly. They deliberately made it difficult for students to take notes. One of them, author of a famous book on law, said to us: 'I will give you examples, but I will not give you the chance to write them down. I do not want you to learn them by heart. I want you to think, to think, to think. Then you must construct your own examples.'

So most students did not attempt to take notes of his lectures. He saw me writing, however. I took down every word, and at home I typed it out. Then I learnt most of it by heart. This lecturer was my personal tutor. Every three weeks I had an interview with him, at which he asked questions. He was surprised that sometimes I could reply in his very words. He asked me about it, and finally I confessed that I knew shorthand. He was not pleased.

What I want to say here is this: I noticed that when I was writing fast shorthand, it was necessary that I should not think about the meaning of what I was hearing and writing. He spoke at about 140 words a minute sometimes. I could just manage to take that down in good shorthand. But if I began to think about what he was saying, my shorthand would become hesitant and faltering. Sometimes he made a joke. If I began to laugh inwardly, I found my writing was checked.

So I learned to pay no attention to the meaning; just to keep the smooth flow from the sound of his voice through my head and into the shorthand of my pen.

At the end of the lecture, I had little idea of what had been said. But I had a full report of it, in excellent shorthand. In the next day or two, I would type it all out.

I found the same thing with typing. If I began to think of the meaning, it would interrupt the even current of the typing. I developed a technique for typing the notes. I put the shorthand notebook on a little music stand just beyond the typewriter. I kept my eyes on it, and typed entirely by touch, without thinking what it meant. When I had finished a lecture (about eight pages) I pinned the sheets together, and had a rest. Then I began to read them. It was like reading a book for the first time, and it was very easy to learn. These early discoveries taught me something about mental efficiency. I realised how many unnecessary thoughts we have, which disturb the important central concentration.

A friend of mine in the Foreign Office told me something similar. In the old days, telegrams came in cipher – that is to say, they were composed of letters that apparently had no meaning. But when an expert used the secret cipher machine, the meaning would become clear, word by word. He himself for a time was Cipher Officer to the Prime Minister. He told me that one time a message came which the Prime Minister was waiting for. It was most important. When the message came, my friend was called to the Prime Minister's room, and he began working on it, with the machine. The Prime Minister was walking up and down impatiently. But then he was called away. He came back just as the long and complicated job was finished. He said: 'Well, what does it say, what does it say?' My friend simply passed him the sheets he had written, saying: 'I don't know, sir.'

The great man looked at him as if he were mad. Then he snatched the sheets and quickly read them. The message was satisfactory, and he gave an order over the telephone. Then he said quietly: 'Why did you say you did not know?' My friend the Cipher Officer told him: 'I never think of the meaning when I am working on these, sir. If I do, it interferes with the concentration needed.' He told me that the Prime Minister stared at him, and then slowly nodded.

Some interpreters have told me the same thing. What is called 'simultaneous interpreting' is a very difficult job. They have to listen to a man talking in, say, French, and translate it and speak it in another language. While they are speaking, they must also listen to the new sentences which the speaker is uttering. It is a great feat of concentration. They have told me that though one must understand the meaning of what is said, one must not think of anything beyond the bare meaning. The translator must not think: 'How will this affect my country?' or 'Perhaps this is all a lie.' If he thinks such thoughts, his concentration will be disturbed. Then he will make mistakes. He must hear the names as if they were the names of unknown people. Nothing to do with him.

Again, my brother was an expert golfer, with a handicap of plus three. He told me that when facing a vital shot, he had learnt to drop from his mind all thoughts of the consequences. 'If I think that I must get a birdie here because otherwise I cannot keep in the lead, my shot will be uncertain. I dismiss all those thoughts, and just think: the shot, the shot, the shot. I visualise a perfect shot, and nothing else.'

Some people say that it is impossible to control the mind. How can a translator listen to the names of his country and its people as if they had nothing to do with him? In an ancient Indian text, the pupil says: 'I think it is impossible to control the thoughts of the mind. It is like trying to catch hold of the wind.' To which the teacher replies: 'It is indeed difficult to control the mind. But by practice, and by learning to be indifferent, it can be done.' The expert translator, and the others, can do it. After years of practice they can detach their minds from everything else.

In the examples given above, we can see that it is necessary to be indifferent, unconcerned, with anything outside the job one is doing. These are special cases, and by practising in these fields, one can become indifferent to other things. But this sort of practice gives that skill only in the one particular field. Many expert golfers, very calm when playing, are unable to control their temper, or nervousness, at other times. The *budo* training was far superior because it was for the whole of life, not just one small part of it.

Specialisation

There is a tendency in life to specialise. That is natural enough: to become a doctor or a lawyer, one has to study and practise for a number of years at different areas in the same general field. To be a good typist or computer operator, you have to become expert on a keyboard.

To type in Japanese *kana-majiri*, one has to learn a much larger keyboard. When Western typists are told about the Japanese keyboard, with the 600 common characters in the middle and the two wings of further characters, and are told that Japanese typists know the position of nearly all of them, we tend to say 'Impossible!' But a good many Japanese manage it.

Specialisation gives us a role in life: most of us earn our living by some kind of specialised skill. Brick-laying is a special skill: Churchill used to build walls in his garden, and he is supposed to have said that to lay bricks perfectly is a fine art, but some people think it must be easy: 'You just spread the cement and put the bricks on it. These are the people who think it must be easy to take the cloth and make a suit from it: you just cut it and sew it.' But tailors and bricklayers must both be highly skilled, or the result is hopeless.

In the *budo* arts, specialisation is accepted as necessary until technique has been learned. But after that, it is a danger. One can become a prisoner of specialisation. And we see this everywhere in life. Specialists develop their skill in one field but then they begin to feel that this one field is everything. So they apply their specialist skill to other fields, where it is not suitable. Often they cannot free themselves from their imprisonment in their speciality. I will give a small but dramatic example.

My eldest brother was an expert boxer. His speciality was a terrific right-hand hook; he won most of his contests with this. He had so specialised in it, that it was natural to him.

My middle brother was an expert golfer, with a beautiful smooth swing. Occasionally we three brothers went for a week's golf together. We had all played a bit when children. The middle brother now gave us a few lessons.

As a judo man, I was able to follow his instructions. 'Golf is a left-handed game,' he told us. 'Think of pulling the club smoothly with your left arm. Forget the right arm and hand; they will do their work automatically and unconsciously.' Though I played infrequently, I soon got my handicap down to six, where it remained for 40 years.

It was quite different with my eldest brother. He was a sportsman, and he could easily imitate a smooth swing with just the club swishing through the air. But when he came to hit a ball, his right hook took over. He would begin with a beautiful smooth action, controlled by the left arm as he had been taught. But just before the club hit the ball, his body would tense and the right hand would give a lightning punch. The blow was strong, but as it was right-handed, the club cut across the ball. The result was a tremendous slice. The ball sailed away to the right, in a quarter circle. I have never seen such a huge slice. The ball would generally go far into the rough, or out of bounds. My brother desperately tried to control his punch, but he could not do it. His speciality had become part of him. He lost dozens of golf balls. In the end he gave up. Instead of the normal stance on the tee, he made a half-turn to the left. When he hit the ball, it would go far to the left, and then come in an impressive curve back to the fairway. But of course his golf was always very wild and he never got a good handicap.

There are many examples of imprisonment in technique even in technique itself. 'The excellence of a thing is its own undoing' is the Chinese phrase of Chuang Tzu: in English it is two words: 'Too good'.

I remember some skilled judo men who specialised in *ashi-waza* (foot technique), and one of them was expert in *tsubame-gaeshi* or 'swallow counter'. He would make an apparently careless step across in front of the opponent, who would automatically make a *de-ashi-*

barai (advanced foot sweep) attack. The expert would make a lighting circle, avoiding the attack and coming up behind the attacker's foot. It would make a brilliant counter. But this same expert was once caught by his own excellence. He laid the trap by making the seemingly careless step in front of the opponent, whose foot came forward for the *ashi-barai*. This set off the *tsubame-gaeshi*. But instead of going for *ashi-barai* , the opponent took his foot up to the knee, and made a sort of *hiza-guruma* (knee-wheel). The knee had no support below it, and the *tsubame-gaeshi* expert was completely trapped and fell heavily.

These are examples of a general principle. We can see it in life. Man has succeeded in developing, whereas other animals have remained prisoners of their specialisation. Man gave up specialisations: our finger-nails were once specialised claws, but we gave up clawing in favour of a general use of the hand. We have given up specialisations of scent, and sensitivity to vibration. We use inference to tell us about our surroundings.

In our own lives too we can see specialists who are imprisoned in their own skill. There are people who are experts at estimating the price of things; when they see a thing, they can at once estimate what its price could be. Or rather, they can estimate what they could buy it for, and then how much profit they could make by selling. But such people can become unable to see anything but price. If they look at a fine picture, they see its beauty, but as an indication of the price. They may think, 'Yes, it is beautiful, but that style of painting is not popular today; the market is down for that sort of thing.' Then they actually lose interest in the picture altogether; it would not be a good investment. They know about the price of things, but not about how to appreciate things in themselves.

A British multi-millionaire once made a striking remark: 'Anyone can make a lot of money, if they are willing to sacrifice everything else for it. Their friends, their marriage, their spare time – everything has to be for the purpose of money. If people knew how narrowing the pursuit of money is, they would not want to devote themselves to it.'

This same millionaire tried to relieve the narrowness of his own life by supporting various charities. For instance, he and some others set up a factory where severely disabled people could earn a living by making toys. One day he visited the factory, and went round the work places. This gave him (as he said) a temporary relief from always thinking about money.

He stopped to watch one young man who had lost some fingers from each hand. This man was slowly and carefully gluing pieces of some coloured material together. He had only just begun this job, and it was not clear what the toy would be. The old rich man bent over and asked in a kindly way:

'What are you making, son?'

The worker looked at him and said: 'A pound an hour.'

Help

At many Zen monasteries, a training week can involve a good deal of strain. A man who felt himself to be a keen Buddhist in a general sense thought he would like to have the experience. So he made inquiries of a Zen teacher as to whether he would be allowed to join in such a week, and if so, what it would involve.

'You may come,' the teacher told him. 'Almost anyone may come if prepared to stick to the rules: there's not much sleep, there's a strict discipline, and you have to be prepared to submit to rough treatment when you are slack. If I think it necessary, you may be required to sign a statement in advance before the local Prefect that you agree to whatever treatment you receive, and will make no complaint then or later.'

The inquirer, a bit taken aback, told him: 'Unfortunately my state of health is such that any severe strain might have the most serious consequences.' He described it briefly. 'So would you consider, in my case, giving up some of the most stringent rules on account of my medical condition?'

'No,' said the teacher. 'It is for you to give up your condition on account of our rules.'

Limits of technique

The time comes when, for one reason or another, even the finest technique fails. In Japan there used to be (and for all I know, there still is) a certain distance, almost an antipathy, between some of the more fanatical judo men and the more fanatical *kendo* (fencing) men. The *kendo* men are supposed to say under their breath, or just think: 'Oh yes, a *kendo* man against a judo man. Well, just pick up a stick (even an umbrella would do) and then one thrust in the throat, and he's finished.' That is what they thought, or what we thought they thought. And on the judo side, we used to look at them and think: 'Yes, and when you haven't got your little stick, what then, eh?'

Each side had stories about the other side. We used to circulate a story about a Japanese policeman who was a fourth Dan at *kendo*; he went with another policeman, a first Dan judo man, to arrest a man who had run amok with a sword. When they came to the house, this man stood in the doorway waving his bloodstained sword. The *kendo* man (so the judo account runs) fainted, and it was left to the judo man to pick up a garden rake and rush the madman, who tripped and was then disarmed.

I don't know what the *kendo* version of this story was, if they had one. But they did have a story about a very famous *jujitsu* expert named Hoshino at the end of the last century. *Jujitsu* is not the same as judo, but for the purpose of the story, the story tellers used to equate them. Well, Hoshino had a dispute with a foreign sailor near the docks at Yokohama. The sailor was drunk, and imagined he could dispose of his small antagonist with one big blow to the jaw. Hoshino easily evaded this, and at once trapped the arm in a lock. He was an expert, and knew how to apply a lock so as to cause slight pain but without injuring the arm seriously. If the man struggles violently, then he causes great pain to himself, the arm is damaged, and in extreme cases broken.

So Hoshino was quite at ease. He knew he was complete master in this familiar situation. There was however a difference. The foreign sailor was fighting drunk, so drunk that he did not feel the pain. He smashed his other fist into Hoshino's jaw, knocking him out. Then he ran off, holding his broken arm to his chest.

I may add that I believe this story to be true, as I heard it from an old *jujitsu* man who had trained in a Yokohama *dojo* (martial arts hall) at that time. I have heard it queried on grounds that a drunken man would still feel pain. However, I have some reason to believe he wouldn't.

My uncle was in the Royal Navy about a century ago and he got a wound in the toe, which had to be amputated. In those days chloroform and ether were coming into use, but he refused to have an anaesthetic. He was my mother's elder brother, and she told me about it. He said that it was cowardly to use such things. So (she told me) he got very drunk on rum, and then four medical students held him firmly. The surgeon cut off the toe very quickly. She was told that he did not struggle, but she was not sure whether that was because of self-control or because of the rum. When I was a child I saw that uncle sometimes. I always wanted to say to him: 'After all, taking a lot of rum is the same thing as having an anaesthetic, isn't it?' But I never dared.

The Hoshino story, and the *kendo* story, illustrate the limits of technique. Sooner or later the time will come when we cannot depend on our trained skills, even if they are very good. Even the monkeys fall off trees, and even Kobo makes a mistake with the brush.

The first Kodokan, an eight-mat *dojo*

Humble

Judo is one of the 'Ways of inner development', and an important element in one's inner development is not to forget the sense of shame. When Dr. Kano founded his judo academy, some of the schools of *jujitsu* contained members who were little more than street fighters; some of these had jobs as debt collectors; they could terrify debtors by a show of violence, and their harsh voices were specially cultivated by them. There is a humorous Meiji song:

> 'When I drink sake,
> Spring opens up in my heart,
> The very debt collectors
> Sound like nightingales!'

Dr. Kano refused membership of the Kodokan to any who engaged in street fighting, and he expelled from the Kodokan any member who had been involved in it. When some of the local toughs found that the Kodokan men were forbidden to fight, they began a campaign of provocation in the street. Some of the masters of judo asked Dr. Kano: 'What are we to do? They are beginning to attack us physically. How can we help defending ourselves?' This was indeed the case – the local bullies, realising that they were on to a good thing, as the saying goes, were assaulting them with impunity. Dr. Kano's reply was a surprise. 'You have two good legs. Use them, and run!'

This was of course a great humiliation. Even famous masters like Nagaoka, Toku and Mifune had occasionally to run away, followed by jeers. They could easily have won in a fight, but they had to run. They mastered their pride and anger. I knew some of them in their latter years; they had an impressive dignity and self-possession. On one occasion Toku ran into a blind alley, and had no escape. He turned on his pursuers, and quickly disposed of five of them. He injured one man badly. The police did not pursue the matter as he was able to prove he had been attacked by them. Nevertheless, Dr. Kano expelled him for six months.

When I knew Toku he had had a stroke, from which he had partially recovered. He was master of the *dojo* at the Kodokan on most days, and was very insistent on politeness and correct behaviour. I saw him correct tiny details of a *zarei* sitting bow six times before he was satisfied and let the student go. Then he sat just inside the door of the dojo, and reprimanded students who came in with a slovenly bow. The word went quickly round the changing rooms: 'The old man's on the warpath!' Then all the students entered with flawless bows.

I often practised with him, if one could call it practice. When he made the slightest movement of the hands in a sort of mock *tewaza* (a hand throw – which was about all he could manage) one simply jumped past him and landed with a crash on the far side. Sometimes one had to hold him up as one went past. All the young fourth and fifth Dans did this with the old teacher of their particular line. It made you part of his school, so to speak, and afterwards you would get a really good practice with one of his pupils, or one of his pupils' pupils. All the tough young men went through this, and in a way it taught them humility – being thrown about by an old man in front of everyone. The idea was to prevent a young expert from swaggering, and with some at least it gradually became effective.

So if you feel that you have to spit in someone's face, probably the safest target will be a seasoned judo man. But not a young man – he may not have mastered himself yet.

Dr. Kano's washing

In the East, a traditional way of washing clothes was to soak them in soapy water, jerk the dirt out of them, rinse and then dry them in the sun. In India the jerk was given by whirling the wet cloth in the air and slapping it down on to a clean flat stone. This does get the dirt out, but does not improve the life of the cloth. In Japan in the last century, they used to pummel the clothes with the fists to do the same thing.

I heard Dr. Kano tell how he had observed the maids in his house doing this. He stopped them, and showed them how to hit the clothes with the edge of the straight hand, the thumb turned in. After a few weeks he gave some more instruction, on how to use the whole body in the blow. He checked their progress from time to time, and some became quite expert at the movement. We should note that he said they were practising the action with attention, not just repeating it mechanically.

He further related how one evening one of them visited a sick parent, and had to return through the Tokyo streets at night. She took a short-cut through a dimly lit street. A young tough jumped out from the shadows, and caught her long sleeve. Without thinking, she found her body instantly turning towards him, and her right arm delivering the same blow it had so often given to the laundry. But this time it was on his outstretched arm. The arm was broken. This was confirmed next day by asking the local bone-setter: 'an unusual injury,' he said.

I heard Dr. Kano give this as an example of what he called in English 'automatic secondary application'; in other words, a movement practised on judo principles which was useful in quite a new situation, and which went into effect simply by the need of the moment, without a conscious decision.

Ingenuity

One of the elements in more advanced stages of the ways is to develop ingenuity. Some of this can be done by the student himself. For instance, in judo he can try practising with one arm tucked inside his belt, so that he has only the other arm to fight with. This will sometimes give him an insight into the true mechanics of a throw, especially if he tends to rely on the strength of his arms to make up for lack of technique. When he has only one arm to use, he can no longer do this, and he has to discover how to use the rest of his body properly.

Some physically strong judo men tend to use one or two techniques which they can force through by their strength. But if they come up against a good technician, who can anticipate and forestall their favourite technique, they fail completely.

I mentally compare them to people who go to a foreign country, and do not study the language properly but master a number of set phrases, sometimes highly colloquial. They often sound impressive for about ten minutes. But after that, they have exhausted their repertoire of phrases, and begin to repeat them. I knew a man who had lived several years in Japan, but who never studied Japanese properly, though he had mastered several foreign languages. He was regarded as an authority on Japan by other foreigners, and in fact did know some rather out of the way things. It was therefore assumed that he must be expert in Japanese language. I knew that in fact his knowledge was very sketchy. We were once at a party when a Japanese professor came up to him, and talked for a little in English. He then said: 'And I have heard that you also know Japanese well.' I found myself wondering what he would say (and also hoping that the same question would not be put to me). When the reply came, it was a masterstroke. He just gave a laugh and jerked out rapidly: 'Zenbu wasurechatta!' He laughed again, and began to talk about something else. It was certainly clever. His statement that he had forgotten everything was in highly colloquial Japanese, which denied what he was saying. The professor looked impressed, and asked no more. The prepared all-purpose response achieved its object.

I saw the same sort of thing from the Japanese side, in my first year in Japan. Some very senior man would agree to brush a Chinese character 'for the foreigner'. The paper and brushes and ink and inkstone were brought with due solemnity, and he would then rapidly write two or three characters, often in the *so-sho*, the difficult Grass Hand. Occasionally he would dash off a sketch in a few strokes. I was always duly awed by his skill; sometimes I showed one to my Japanese teacher and asked him about it. He generally said it was well done, though I detected sometimes a slight reservation. Anyway, my general impression was that the senior ranks of *budo* men, and also company presidents, were all masters of calligraphy.

But in my second year the bubble burst. I saw the same company president write for someone else. To my amazement, he brushed the same two characters which he had brushed for me: *tetsu-shi*, or iron will. The character for iron, which was then much more complicated than it is today, was written with just the same *so-sho* strokes. I realised that this was what in England we used to call our 'party piece'. One was not expected to be able to do anything else in the same field.

My mother was brought up, like other girls at the turn of the century, to play the piano. She was almost tone deaf, and music meant little to her. But she could play one or two pieces quite effectively. They were her 'party pieces'. There are certain piano pieces which sound difficult, but are in fact rather easy to play; some of the girls in those times learnt a few of these, to give the impression that they were skilful pianists. But in fact they could not play anything else.

These things are examples of ingenuity. I do not say that they are wrong. After all, very few company presidents in countries outside Japan could do anything like the party piece of the Japanese president or senior. Nor would they be asked to. The fact that Japanese are asked, and admired when they can do it, is an example of the high cultural level in Japan. The mild deception involved is not really a deception, because most people know about it. And after all, even if these *so–sho* characters are the only ones which he can write, at least they are well done. But one cannot live by ingenuities like this. The man who relies on certain tricks in life, like the one who relies on mere tricks in judo, may have success for a time, but it cannot last long. The test of the company president is not whether he can write a couple of Chinese characters well, but whether he can make his company a success, socially as well as financially. And the test of the judo man is whether he can develop the principle of maximum efficiency (*saidai-noritsu*) in his physical and mental undertakings and the principle of mutual benefit in his social life. The true use of ingenuity is to develop methods of self–training to achieve these aims.

It is important not to follow established methods without studying whether they can be further developed. It is important not simply to go on imitating a teacher. When as a small child I showed a talent for the piano, my father found for me a well-known teacher. He was an elderly man, himself the pupil of a famous pianist called Oskar Beringer. In the 19th century, when Beringer flourished, it was thought that the best way to train students was to teach them to keep the back of the hand level all the time; the work was done by the fingers alone. I practised with him for some years. One exercise he set was to play scales with a matchbox resting on the back of each hand. If it fell off, that was a bad fault. When the thumb passes under the other fingers, it is quite difficult to keep the back of the hand level. I developed a method of doing it by curving the hands inwards a little, which seemed to make it easier to pass the thumb. The teacher made no comment.

After a couple of years, when I had made good progress, my father (a professional musician himself) took me to a new teacher, who had been a noted virtuoso in his time.

At my first lesson, he said: 'Why do you hold your hands like that ?' 'It's easier to get the thumb under while I keep my hand level,' I replied. I added proudly, 'I can keep a matchbox on my hands when I play scales.' 'What for?' he said. I felt bewildered, and at the same time furious. I thought how hard I had practised to achieve this very thing, which was now brushed aside. He saw this, and put his hand on my shoulder as he said: 'Look. Mozart used to play that way, and the practise you've done is not wasted. But these days we play with a more relaxed hand; you can throw your hand up to pass the thumb under.'

Then I felt better. Of course he must have met the same situation many times before. But it was a good lesson for later life: a good traditional way of doing things may not be the only way. When we have made good progress in basic skills, we can look out for opportunities to exercise ingenuity.

Most people polish a table using only one hand; but the best way for physical development is to use both hands, a cloth in each. Similarly I have mentioned elsewhere how Dr. Kano taught the maids in his house to strike the wet clothes with the edge of the hand, and using a movement of the whole body. There is still scope for ingenuity in simple things of life: most people all over the world hold a pen in a strong grip near the tip, as they did when they were small children. But the best place to hold it is two inches from the tip, as a high speed shorthand reporter does. Then you don't have to keep moving the hand with almost every word.

The tradition of judo

In the Japanese *budo* tradition there are many particular 'Ways': *kendo*, the way of the sword; *shodo*, the way of the brush; *kyudo*, the way of the archer, and many others. Even other branches of culture, for instance music, have a connection with *budo*. An expert in the *koto* (a sort of horizontal harp), or the *chanoyu* (tea ceremony) always keeps a posture correct from the *budo* standpoint. That is to say, if he or she were suddenly attacked, their balance would be perfect so that there could be an instant response (not necessarily of a martial kind).

I myself watched the once-a-year tea ceremony demonstrated at Daitokuji by the then Master of the Ura-senkei school, and I also often watched Michio Miyagi the koto master. I noted that from the judo point of view their posture was always kept in balance.

We judo men believe that judo has a special meaning in *budo*, because the judo man has nothing but himself. He has no sword, bow, tea-kettle, or writing brush. His training is general, not tied to specific implements. So the idea is that it forms a basic training in using body-mind in unspecified ways, in preparation for using them in specific ways.

The other view is that the best way to learn how to use the body-mind is to practise some limited expression, and from that gradually extend the principles that have been learnt. However, the judo men point out that some people become relatively skilful in some limited field, without really mastering anything more than skill in that field. For instance, many children learn how to write quite effectively without ever learning to keep a good balance while they are writing, or even how to hold the pen efficiently.

Judo koan

This is one of the most complicated of the ways, and perhaps the nearest to life. It is a general training of the body and not concentration on a special aim with special instruments. But because of the complexity of the technique, many students become wholly absorbed in technical achievement, losing the one principle in study of the individual tricks.

In judo there is no complete rest at all; always the balance has to be actively preserved under the push and pull of the opponent. The student is expected to find the truth of the Taoist saying: 'The stillness is not the real stillness; only when there is stillness in movement does the universal rhythm manifest.'

In the series of photographs on the next page the attacker (on the right) finds a small chance and comes in. At the crucial moment the opponent will either shift his right foot forward to take his weight, or keep it still (steps 2 or 6). If he moves his right foot, then the throw (series A) will succeed, and the throw (series B) fails; if he does not move, then B will suceed and A will fail. The difficulty is that if we wait to see which he will do, we shall hesitate, and the rhythm of the movement will be lost. (The complete whirling action of B takes only about a second). If we do not hesitate but go in blindly, we are liable to find ourselves attempting the wrong throw.

As in most of these *koan* (spiritual riddle), there is a sort of cheating method by which we can half solve the problem. Suppose we have tried B and succeeded; when we come in again in the same way, the other man will probably expect B again, and this time he will move his right foot. If we anticipate this, we can go smoothly into the other throw. Then next time we change again. Simple alteration is of course

A

B

2

1

6

1. Attacker (on the right) is about to swing his left leg forward.

A

2. If opponent braces his right leg by stepping forward...
3. attacker takes his left foot forward and plants it down...
4. swings his right leg through...
5. and throws opponent to the *rear.*

3

7

B.

6. If opponent leaves his right foot where it is...
7. attacker swings his left leg in front...
8. whirls his body round and down...
9. and throws opponent to the front.

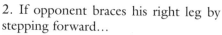

4

The koan: If you anticipate one alternative, but he takes the other, the throw is blocked. If you wait to see what he does, you hesitate and spoil the throwing action. If you make your mind a blank your body will not move. How to solve the problem?

8

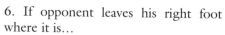

5

9

too obvious for success, but good results can be obtained by determining in advance a sequence like A-B-A-A-A or A-B-B-B-A and so on. Still the problem is not solved. By determining our action in advance we get the advantage of smooth uninterrupted movement, but often we shall still be trying the wrong throw and be doomed to fail.

There is a song of the Way on the point:

> *The trees on the mountain are not so thick*
> *That from time to time a moonbeam*
> *Cannot penetrate.*

Perhaps we can find an intellectual application of this verse to the problem, but unless it can help us to find a solution in practice, we cannot be said to understand it.

Beginners

One of my early lessons in the spirit of judo came when I had been practising for about six months. I was sitting on the edge of the mat, watching two beginners take their grading contest. Watching them was a boring business, and I was whispering to my next door neighbour about something else. I knew there was nothing to be learnt from a couple of absolute beginners. The referee, who was also my teacher, was walking round the mat as referees do. My neighbour had just said something a bit funny, and I was grinning as I half turned and whispered back to him. Suddenly I felt a kick in my side. We are not used to that sort of thing, and I nearly got up and walked out of the place. Still, I was very keen on judo, and I managed to go on sitting as if nothing had happened, but inwardly fuming.

After the contests were all over, this Japanese teacher came up to me. I imagined several things he might say, but I could never have imagined what he did actually say. It was: 'You think you have nothing to learn from beginners – but I learn from them. I study their judo. Sometimes one of them has, naturally, a very good movement, from which I can learn. Don't think you can't learn too.'

It was some years before I fully understood what he meant. The realisation came slowly. Some time after that incident I was again watching from the edge of the mat when the two names were called for a contest. One man was big and strong, but clumsy; the other was wiry and fairly skilful, but much lighter. (In those days there were no weight categories). The same tutor was there, but this time he was not the referee, and we were standing together by the side of the mat. He said to me: 'Which one do you think will win?' I had no idea at all, and said so. He said: 'The light one will be able to control the big one for a few minutes;

then when the big one gets tired, the other one will throw him.' It happened just as he said. The big one plunged about like an elephant, but the thin one managed to survive all the attacks. Then after about four minutes, the big one began to slacken, and the lighter one managed to catch him with an *ouchi-gari* (minor inner-reap).

The teacher told me afterwards: 'You don't know which side is going to win because you don't study. You only think of your own judo. And while you go on like that, your judo will be useless.' I was not very pleased at this comment, but I began to see the force of it. When I began to try to predict the result of a contest, I realised how shallow my judo knowledge and judgement were. I never did get much good at it, though I made some progress.

Some judo champions do not study the judo of others. So they can teach only pupils whose physique and movement are just like their own. To become a good teacher, one must be interested in the potentialities of judo practised by all kinds of *judoka* (judo players) and not just what is effective for one particular type.

Kind-hearted

I knew well a judo man who was a fine technician and strategist on the mat, but he was too kind-hearted. At least, that is the only way I can describe his attitude in important contests. He seemed to be thinking: 'If I beat this chap, who has come here with such great hopes, he'll be very discouraged and depressed. It probably means so much to him, whereas I don't really care if I just draw with him.' We used to say to him: 'Look, that chap doesn't want your kindness. He wants you to go all-out. Against a better man, he wants to fail: then he'll improve. He's come here to fail.' But nothing we said made any difference: he was too nice, he was too kind.

Well, just before he went on the mat for one big contest, the teacher took him out of the hall, into a corner, saying he had something to tell him. (He spoke about this later, to a few close friends. That was in strict confidence, but it's a long time ago now). When they were alone and no-one could see, the teacher spat in his face. It's a nasty experience. He said he just stood there, dumbfounded.

The teacher produced a little towel and wiped his face clean, and led him by the arm back to the hall, where his name was just being called. 'Go on,' he said, 'go on.' To general surprise, this man who usually went to the centre of the mat very politely, now strode on with a face like iron. He won in almost no time.

It must be emphasised that this was a very exceptional case. Being kind–hearted is not exactly a weak point, but it is against the spirit of contest, which requires one to fight very hard. The basis of judo is peace, and there is peace and friendship before and after the contest. But during the contest, the two are taking the role of intense rivalry and competition. There is still an underlying peace, which shows itself in the fact that they keep to the rules even in the keenest contest, but within those rules they may and must try everything in order to win.

As Dr. Kano said, the battle is not fought with hatred or enmity. In some old texts the opponent is called *teki* (enemy), but Dr. Kano never used the term *teki*, but rather *aite*, which means the one who faces you, and includes the sense of both partner and opponent. There are no personal feelings, either of hatred or of over-kindness.

The case I have described was very exceptional, and the teacher used a very exceptional method. It cannot be recommended generally, and I doubt whether Dr. Kano would have altogether approved of it. It was effective, but I feel he would have found some other way.

A Japanese Zen rock garden

Hard and soft

In one of the traditional scrolls of *budo* martial arts, there is a poem:
Do not meet hard with hard, or soft with soft,
There is no result and it is meaningless,
Catch the flung stone with a cloth,
Pin the wind-fluttered cloth with a stone.
These general principles, and the poetic metaphors which illustrate them, can be a help in life. But they have to be understood.

There are people who live always by hardness: they are fighters, pushers, shouters. If you meet them with fighting, pushing and shouting, there is no real result. You may defeat them for a time, but they are not convinced and will seek revenge. They will constantly oppose all you try to do, and can hold it up and limit it.

Then there are people who live entirely by softness. At the first little difficulty or opposition in anything, they change course, or give up entirely. If you meet their feebleness by making no demands on them, again nothing gets done and there is no result.

We have to learn how to neutralise and contain the forceful without directly opposing them with force, and we have to learn how to rouse the indecisive and hold them to a decision. It has to be done internally, not only externally. We have to learn how to contain the anger and will to dominate, but not by forcible restraint; and how to energise our inertia or timidity without any concessions to 'human weakness'.

The poem shows that we must be able to use both hard and soft, and that we skilfully use hard against soft, and soft against hard. It is a sort of inspirational skill, and inspiration does not come into a disturbed mind. It arises in a mind that has been calmed by meditation. The skill may not be obvious: sometimes the soft is concealed in the hard, or vice versa. How does it work in practice? There has to be a concrete example, and from a judo man it is natural that the example should be from that training.

So here it is. There are technical exercises which judo students of some years perform together. One of them is to lie face-down on the mats, and then pull oneself forward by the forearms, pressing them on the mats and then pulling in. The body slides along; the feet trail behind. It is easy at first, but soon gets tiring. They are made to do it three times round a large hall, which takes many to near the limit of exhaustion. The teacher watches carefully. If one of them is going 'Ooh!' or 'Aaagh!' he knows that man is not really tired: if he has energy to say 'Ooh!' or 'Aaagh!' he has got something to spare. But if in the third round the teacher sees one man, very quiet, suddenly going pale, he knows that man ought to stop.

There is however a difficulty. The united effort of will must not be broken. What keeps many people going during these periods of exhaustion is the knowledge that others are doing the same thing, enduring the same hardship, mastering the body by will. If one man is taken out and allowed to rest, that unity is liable to collapse. 'I'm just as tired as he is, why shouldn't I...' The teacher must prevent that.

He gives a shout of simulated anger, jumps forward, picks up the man by collar and belt, and slings him down in the middle.

'Why don't you do it properly?' he shouts. 'I've told you again and again. Look at the angle of my arms here...' he demonstrates. 'Now look and see how I'm making the pull. You're doing it unevenly... always think you know better... don't listen...' It can be quite a tongue-lashing. The others keep on steadily, glad it is not them. 'Now get back, and do it properly.'

The man begins again. He has been reprimanded, scolded, humiliated, but he has had a little rest. And in the next day or two, the teacher invites him to have a coffee with him.

This is an example of the soft concealed in the hard.

Irrelevancies

When I was training in Japan, I knew a senior judo man who was expert in groundwork *newaza*, and especially armlocks. He was a small thin man, with very supple and wiry legs, and he could always somehow thread one through the gaps and wind it round the other man's arm. Then he would put the lock on very fast. He was not an official teacher, but he used to go nearly every day to the Kodokan and practise his extraordinary technique.

Some people used to watch him, but not from close up, because he would suddenly end that practice, and then call on the nearest man to go on with him. A splendid chance, one might think. Yet not many liked to take the opportunity. The reason was that there was something about him that was just a little vicious. He would put the lock on very quickly, and to the limit. With his great experience, he knew just how far to go. But when the opponent tapped surrender, he would not release him immediately, but keep the lock on and increase it fractionally. He did not injure the arm; as far as I know, he never injured anybody. But it gave just a tiny bit of pain. Then he would let it go. So to practise with him meant having to endure these little shots of pain. The joint was not damaged at all; it was just slightly unpleasant, and people avoided practising with him if they could. He would sometimes give a little instruction on one of the locks, but there again, the pupil had to go through this experience, and few volunteered for a lesson, though there was so much to be learned from him.

I had the same feeling myself, after a few such experiences with him. I did not want to practise with him; he was vicious. Then something in me said: 'You can learn from him some things which you could not get elsewhere.' To that, I produced one of those high ethical arguments which are often used to hide fear: 'I ought not to practise with him, because I might get infected by his viciousness.' The inner conversation went on:

'Am I vicious myself ? After all, I have done spiteful things.' 'No, I can't be, because I dislike it so much in him.' 'Oh but they say it is just one's own unconscious fault that seems so odious in others.'

So finally I decided to learn from him regularly; perhaps I'd infect him instead of him infecting me. He seemed a bit surprised when I began coming up regularly for a lesson. At first I had the impression that he was putting the last little pressure on a bit more. Foreigners were then a rarity in judo circles. We were known to be extraordinary, and he may have felt that perhaps we did not feel pain in the usual way. When I kept coming back, his attitude changed. He even forgot sometimes to put that last pressure on. He did teach me a good deal. Some of it I could not use myself, because our physical build was so different. But it enabled me later on to teach those who were of his physical type.

The whole experience was a useful lesson for life. He had this unpleasant characteristic, but the little discomfort was really nothing to a judo man. It had nothing to do with the fact that I could learn some unusual techniques from him. I had nearly been put off by something quite irrelevant. How often in life we hear someone say something to the effect that they had made a good start at school with French, or mathematics, 'but then I moved up to a new class where I didn't like the teacher. He was supposed to be very good at teaching his subject, but he made one or two remarks about my accent (I'm from the West country, you know), and I couldn't stand him. I made no progress, and it put me off for life.'

There is a saying: 'Great obstacles can be wrestled with and defeated, but not trivialities, because there is nothing to catch hold of.' Or as another tradition puts it: 'It is not so much your great passions as your silliness that really holds you up.'

Ippon-yari

The way to progress is: give up one's *ippon-yari*, one's strongest throw, for a time. The pupil who does this will look weak, until he gradually develops other techniques. People will laugh at him perhaps. They will say: 'Oh, he cannot do much now; his old *ippon-yari* does not work any more, so he has given it up. And he cannot do much else.' It takes great courage to be laughed at for two or three months by opponents whom one could easily defeat. One is not allowed to defeat them, because the *ippon-yari* is barred. Not many young judo men can do it, unless there is the support of a teacher.

I can remember how when I was third Dan, I was tall and strong, and had a good *harai-goshi* (sweeping hip) which no one in the *dojo* could stop. Then the teacher said: 'Don't use that for two months.' He made it even more difficult by adding: 'Develop *ko-uchi* and *o-uchi*. Just use those.' He knew that I was getting very conceited about my judo ability.

The next two months were humiliating. The others soon found that I was using only *ko-uchi* and *o-uchi*, and so they simply kept their feet close together. I failed again and again and again. Of course this would have made a *harai-goshi* very easy, but I was not allowed to use that. So I had to develop some strategies to make them take a wide step occasionally. In the end I did get quite skilful at these two throws. Without the humiliation of those repeated failures, I could not have done so. (But after the two months, I did enjoy myself with *harai-goshi*.)

I have experienced the value of this sort of training in life generally. When I was small, I used to argue with my elder brother. I say argue, but in fact we just shouted at each other, interrupting all the time. As a student I used the same method, and because I was a judo man I could often seem to win an argument. The opponent would be cowed into silence.

Sometimes my argument was quite reasonable, but still I tended to shout it. That was my *ippon-yari*. Then I heard Dr. Kano say, in a lecture: 'The right way is not to try to overbear an opponent by force of wealth, or position in society, or physical force. He may become silent, but he will not be convinced. The right way is to use reasoning to convince him.' From that time I began to give up my habit of shouting, and developed the art of arguing sensibly. It improved my life and reputation. Without that instruction from a respected teacher, I doubt whether I would have learnt it. Certainly my brother did not: in his vigorous old age, it still remained his favourite method of debating a point.

There is also instruction given by a teacher unconsciously, without a word. He teaches by his behaviour. I once saw a very neurotic man come to The Budokwai for lessons, who became very upset when he was told that first he must learn how to fall. He said, 'I have come to learn how to throw, not how to fall.' The teacher, Yukio Tani, went across to him quietly and said: 'You want to throw others. But they will have to fall when you throw them. So they must learn how to fall. Do you think you should be the only one who does not know how to fall?'

The man looked furious. He thought he was being mocked. He tried to slap Mr. Tani's face. The teacher checked the blow, but did nothing else. He just stood there calmly. We young pupils were furious and were going to throw the man out, but a senior member waved us back and said to him quietly: 'You do not know how to behave, sir.' He took him by the arm to the changing room, and then out of the *dojo*. The teacher never referred to the matter, and I was very impressed by the perfect self-control shown by him and the senior member. They did not seem even to be angry. They treated this unbalanced man as if he were a small child in a tantrum. That was a surprise to me.

Run-up

To deliver the cricket ball, the bowler has to make a long run-up. He runs towards the wicket, and then bowls the ball. With this method, he can make it fly much faster than anyone can do from a standing position. Similarly, the golfer needs a backswing for his drive, and a boxer needs some space to develop a big punch. If there is no space, it is only a push, not a punch. The judo man makes a *tsuri-komi* action to hold the opponent off balance while he himself swings into his throw.

To know this principle can be a great help in life. Big emotional disturbances do not come suddenly; they need a little time to build up their force. The mind can be trained to recognise them while they are still in the early stages.

When we hear some insulting remark about ourselves, in the first few seconds it is often clear that the words are simply the result of jealousy, or mindless spite, or to please someone else. At this moment, it is easy to shrug them off. They are trivial, often pathetic.

The dogs bark, but the caravan moves on. We do something else at once, and it is easy to forget. If however the mind is allowed to stick with them, they seem to develop a deeper meaning. Then they become important. Resentment, and then anger, arise.

It is essential to see clearly the early stages, and at once turn away.

A man in an embassy, who is in debt, is approached by the government of the country with a request for some information. In fact, this piece of information is already in the newspapers in his home country, and he sees no harm in selling it to them. They pay handsomely.

Next time it is for some information which he knows will become public anyway the next day: it seems harmless. But he has been secretly photographed with the agent, and his bank account would not stand inspection. He is in the net. He did not recognise the early signs.

I need to spot the backswing of the passion as it prepares its blow. Then I must move quickly to break the causal chain. A very simple thing may suffice; one teacher recommended taking a drink of cold water. The blow may indeed be delivered, but I shall not be there.

Sacrifices

Some who are attracted to the idea of doing some inner training take it up enthusiastically at first, but become half-hearted when they understand what is required.

'Three hours a day?' they cry. 'Oh surely not. That would mean sacrificing so much. No TV watching, no cinema, very little social life – it sounds so depressing.'

This was put to a teacher, who remarked: 'You look at it from the wrong side. What you have to give up are mostly trivialities. Consider what you have to gain.'

'But there will always be a hankering to enjoy oneself, even if they are trivialities.'

The teacher said: 'Not at all. Come with me to the local judo *dojo*.'

They went together, and the teacher asked the *dojo* master if they could have a word with one of the promising pupils. A young boy came across and stood in front of them. 'How much do you practise?' the teacher asked.

'I get two hours in every day at the school *dojo*, and in the evenings and Sundays I come here. It's all the time I can fit in.'

'But don't you regret giving up watching TV or the cinema, or going out with friends?' inquired the teacher.

The boy stared at him with a puzzled frown. 'What are you talking about?' he said. 'Excuse me, I want to get back,' and he turned away to the mats.

Special duties

Foreign tourists often say how safe they feel in the cities of Japan. The police seem to be everywhere; you walk or drive for five minutes, and you are sure to see a policeman, in his blue uniform and white belt. That he has a gun is noticed by British tourists but not by others; after all, the French for a policeman is *gendarme*, which means literally 'an armed man', just like the old Italian and Spanish word *carabiniero*. The tourist in Japan is careful about his behaviour; there always seems to be a policeman looking at him. If he becomes a resident, one day he gets a little surprise. He notices that some of these policemen are in fact life-size models. They are very realistic. Still, he can work out a strategy. Suppose he wants to park his car for just ten minutes. He sees a place, but it is a no parking zone, and there is a policeman nearby. He drives slowly round and round for a few minutes, glancing at the policeman every few seconds. When he sees that he does not move at all, he knows that it is a model, and he parks his car and gets away safely. He is pleased with his own cleverness.

Soon afterwards, in the same situation, he observes the motionless model for a minute or so, and then parks his car right under its nose. It then arrests him, and he is fined. Japanese policemen are trained to stand motionless for ten minutes or so. It is not only that the models look like the policemen, but the living policemen look like the models.

Though there is less crime on the streets in Japan, the rare riots when they do occur are much more violent than anything in Britain: the rioting students of 1968 took over, and defended for months, important buildings. The riot police in Japan are specially trained, especially in judo; they do not normally carry guns. I was told about one of their training months by one who had recently passed through it. He said it was very severe, occasionally taking the men to the point of exhaustion and near collapse.

However, in the third week the training authorities seemed to realise that it was perhaps going too far, and they suddenly announced at the end of the morning session that the rest of the day would be free. The trainees could change into their civilian clothes and go into the town. 'You can do as you like,' they were told, ' but you have got to be back here by ten. Then straight to sleep and up early tomorrow. I know it's been tough,' the head trainer concluded sympathetically, 'and I've decided you're entitled to a little break.

They were overjoyed, and set out jauntily together after lunch. The superintendent gave them a friendly wave, and even the craggy face of the judo master had a wintry smile. They had gone about a hundred yards when there was a sudden call: 'Hey, come back! There's something else.'

When they got back they were told that the trip was cancelled; they had to change back into judo kit, and practise hard that afternoon and evening. It was a shattering experience. Somehow they got through the rest of the training month. At the end, the superintendent said he regretted having had to do this, but added: 'You will one day realise the value of it.'

The man who described the experience to me added: 'He was right. Twice in my time with the riot police I have had the experience of being on duty all day and night, and then again the next day. I was just getting ready to fall into bed when a sudden emergency call came, and I had to get into uniform again and go on duty. I was able to do this without too much upset because I had been through that crushing disappointment in the training month.'

As he said this, his face took on that nostalgic expression with which Japanese often relate sufferings of the past. It always reminds me of a half-remembered proverb from *shogi*, (Japanese chess) which goes something like this:

'*Aite no nikusa wa shitashii*'.

It's difficult to translate this into English: 'The very hatefulness of the opponent is dear' does not seem right. The nearest to the thought might be: 'He always gives one a good fight'.

But it sounds better in Japanese.

Excuses

When relative beginners have a little string of successes, it is sometimes the first time in their lives that they have distinguished themselves in their own eyes. They do not realise that there is a good deal of luck in such contests, but feel that now they are on the highroad to success. They often become slack in training.

I saw one such member of a judo club have a rough awakening. He had gone into the monthly grading contest with an air of confidence. He was decisively thrown almost at once. The next day he apologised to the teacher for his poor performance. 'I was rather off colour yesterday,' he said. 'That's why I lost. I'm sorry.' He went on to explain just how he had felt. The teacher looked at him without much interest. 'You didn't lose that contest yesterday,' he said coldly. 'You lost it in the whole month before, when you weren't training properly. And you're losing next month's contest now, today, while you stand here making excuses when you ought to be practising!'

The dragon mask I

With age, a judo expert's speed begins to decline and he has to find means to offset this against up and coming opponents. One of them is to establish a psychological ascendancy over a younger man who may be actually stronger in fighting ability.

This can be done by preventing the junior from estimating the respective standards of ability. An experienced man can make an estimate easily in most cases by merely looking at the movement, but a young man generally cannot do it without something definite to work on, and he can be prevented from getting the information.

The senior's attacking policy is to attempt to throw only when it is certain to succeed - in other words, never to fail in a throw. This often means waiting for quite a time till the opponent takes some risk and so gives an opportunity. But promising young judo men take risks all the time; they get bored unless they are trying something. The senior's defending policy is never to take any risk himself,, so that the opponent never scores. This is not difficult for a patient man.

The physical result of these policies is that in a practice of say six minutes, the junior makes dozens of attempts but does not score at all, whereas the senior makes perhaps three attempts and each time with success. The psychological result is that the senior appears invincible. Every time he attempted a throw, he succeeded. Reason may urge that after all he did not try more than three throws in six minutes. But perhaps he did not want to. Who is to say? The lower grade feels helpless.

A seasoned judo expert has experienced this situation from both sides and knows that in spite of attempts to reason away the conviction of helplessness, it remains very powerful. He sometimes wonders how he could have been taken in by it for so long as a young man, and he wonders why the young men whom he impresses today do not simply see through it.

The paralysing awe of the senior can go on for a good time till one day the senior tries a throw and fails. Immediately, the situation changes; the junior realizes that under certain circumstances he can successfully resist the attack. He now has a measure – out of four attacks in the practice, he has resisted one. The magic spell is broken, and the higher grade appears as a mortal with weaknesses of his own. Once there is a measure, the young man's ambition comes up with confidence – 'now I can only stop one in four, but I will fight to make it one in three and then finally I'll be able to stop them all.'

The essence of the matter is that previously he did not know how wide was the gap between them, and so he could have no ambition of closing it, but now he has a way of measuring it and confidence that it can be reduced and them annihilated.

The same principle applies in struggles against interior enemies. If someone is irrationally afraid of aeroplanes or electric machines, or figures, or getting up in the morning, he tends to regard these things as unconquerable. In such a case, it is essential to make a space in life and establish one clear success. A student can put aside one week during which he is prepared to change his life. During that week he may support his resolution by reading up statistics, if his intellect is one that puts up this sort of argument; he can find out, for instance, that it is safer to travel by plane than by car. If it is a question of getting up in the morning, the resistance is more like to take the form of a headache or stomach-ache. Then the important thing is to go on into the day with the headache or any other ache; it is only for a week, but it does have to be for that week.

After a week of getting up early, or practising rapid adding, or planning and executing an air trip to another part of the country, or getting someone to give a lesson on an electric circuit, the awe-inspiring magical threat of these things disappears. It may not be necessary to go further with them. The point is, that if it is necessary now or later, he is able to do it by a reasonable effort. He is not shrinking back before he has even tried.

In Zen, this is called by various names, and one of them is 'hitting through the dragon mask'. Students of Zen are made to practise a good deal of austerity, and one purpose is to get them used to hitting the dragon masks and finding out that they are only cardboard after all. Experiences of this kind in small things give confidence when it comes to hitting the final dragon mask.

Total commitment: Guy Auffray (France)
throws Hansen (Denmark) with *harai-goshi*
at the world championships in Vienna, 1975. (Photo: David Finch)

The dragon mask II

When I was practising judo at the Kodokan in 1940, Japan and Britain were moving nearer and nearer to war. There was fairly widespread belief in Japan that they were being encircled by potential enemies. I experienced hardly any hostility on the personal level. There was, however, one man at the Kodokan, a tough young fifth Dan, who from the first looked at me in what seemed a baleful way. I will call him K.

When we practised, it was indeed very rough. I came to feel that he had the intention of injuring me, and I suppose I fought back with corresponding aggressiveness. We did not often score points off each other, but it was certainly a rough business. K was a grim-looking fellow, who shaved about once a week (as it was then a patriotic duty to save razor-blades). I began to feel that I did not want to practise with him, as I learnt nothing. However, I felt it would be some sort of moral defeat to refuse him when he came up and asked for a practise in his challenging way. I felt somehow that I had to practise with him every day. Sometimes I would get him over by going up to him at the beginning of the afternoon. At other times I would put it off, and half hoped that K would leave early. But he never did.

Sometimes we would be among the last twenty or thirty on the mats. He seemed to know that I couldn't refuse him, and he would stand there looking at me with sombre satisfaction, waiting to have another go at me. This went on for quite a time. Then one day another fifth Dan, a good friend of mine, said to me:

'You always practise with K, don't you? Every day, don't you?' I felt somehow a bit embarrassed, I didn't know why.

'Well, yes,' I replied, 'I suppose I do.' He gave a little laugh.

'He is afraid of you,' he said.

When I got over my surprise, I realised that I never had to practise with K again. I did not go up to him, and when he came across to me, I turned him down. When he got over his surprise, I think it was as big a relief to him as it was to me.

Yukio Tani (top) and Gunji Kiozumi, the original teachers of The Budokwai

Onshi

To translate *onshi* there is no single word in English. 'revered teacher', 'beloved teacher': these are not natural English phrases. The single word 'teacher' can refer to anyone from Verrocchio who taught Leonardo da Vinci, to an irritable old lady forcing spelling into unwilling children. Master can mean the head of an Oxford college (e.g. Master of Balliol College) or a barber with one apprentice boy. Some continental languages do make more of a distinction: 'maestro' for instance, means a master pianist or artist who also teaches, and quite a different word is used for an employer. In English we borrow the Italian word 'maestro' with that meaning. I suppose this shows that though we have respect for art and learning and science, we do not revere them or their teachers.

Recently, a new word has been introduced to fill the gap, but again it is a foreign word: *guru*. Originally this is a Sanskrit word. Literally, it means 'heavy', and the English 'gravity' comes from the same root. It is used now to mean a very wise adviser, not an employee. Professor Walters was called Prime Minister Thatcher's financial guru. She took his advice without question. But there is no evidence that she revered him.

The traditional Indian guru taught free, but the pupils lived in his house as servants. The awe of his holiness secured absolute obedience, though an ancient Manu lawbook does say that where necessary a stick may be used. There could be a guru of archery of painting, but there was always a spirit of reverence. A famous Indian artist, this century, had a promising pupil. He encouraged him to hold an exhibition of his work. It was much praised. A British critic stood before one picture and said to the young painter: ' You have your own style. But this one you have painted almost in the style of your teacher. And I must say, it is better than his pictures.' The young painter ripped the canvas down and tore it up, saying: 'It is not my aim that anyone should think I surpass my teacher.'

At sixteen, I began training under two traditional Japanese judo teachers in London. One was Yukio Tani, whose grandfather had been a *jujitsu* teacher and had demonstrated before the then Shogun. The other was Gunji Koizumi, an artist and a man of deep culture. His book on Japanese lacquer, for instance, is a classic.

Tani was a small man and his spectacular feats at the beginning of this century, in defeating big wrestlers and boxers, surrounded him, and judo generally, with a magical aura. In general, his methods were kindly, but a few promising pupils faced *fun-kotsu-sai-shin* – translated for us (not by him) 'as grinding the bones and pulverising the flesh'.

So I had some experience of strict learning and teaching before I went to Japan. And I had invented a few austerities of my own. For ten years I never took a hot bath or shower (though I used hot water, reluctantly, to shave). I was quite able to stand under ice-cold showers at the Kodokan and other *dojos* for several minutes without flinching. But outside judo, I had a few surprises. I studied Japanese with a teacher at the Kokusai Gakuyukai and later at the British Embassy. We used the Japanese primary school readers. I remember noticing the character for *oshieru*, to teach. The *hen* radical was a contracted form of *oi*, an old man. The right-hand side *tsukuri* was 'to strike', and at the bottom was the character for a child. So the character for 'teach' was: 'an old man hits the child'. I asked the Japanese teacher whether this was still the idea of teaching and he looked embarrassed and said: 'Oh no, these Chinese characters are very old, and in those days...'

But some years later I met an old Buddhist priest who told me that when he was a boy he had learnt the *sen-ji-mon*, the thousand-character classic, from the same copy that had been used to teach his father and grandfather. He said to me: 'On some pages there were marks of tears, and not only that: some had the marks of blood. When I saw these, it made me study very hard!'

When I heard this, I thought of a school exercise book written by my grandfather when he was about eight. My mother had kept it as a souvenir. It consisted of simple sums: all the answers were correct, most beautifully written, with black and red underlining for the totals. She told me that in those days, at the end of every lesson, the children had to write out perfectly the sums as corrected by the teacher in a perfect copy. It often took about fifteen minutes. If they made a mistake, they had to stay behind after school and write it all out again, but correctly. This was supposed to be a training not only in accuracy, but in neatness, and perseverance also.

Tani and Koizumi were founders of judo in Europe. Their club, The Budokwai, dated from 1918. They were determined to keep a good standard and a good *dojo* atmosphere. At that time there were a number of fake teachers who claimed to teach the secrets of *jujitsu* for large fees. They gave their lessons in private; no one was allowed to watch.

One day, a young man, with an older companion, visited The Budokwai. The young man wanted to join. The older man said he had already learnt judo from a private teacher: 'But my young friend cannot afford that amount of money, so he will have to learn here where the subscription is cheap.'

He watched the *dojo* practise with a contemptuous smile and remarked to the secretary: 'This is just the surface of judo. You fellows do not know the secrets.' The secretary was annoyed and invited him to go on the mat and try out his secrets. 'Oh certainly,' said the man. 'but I am pledged to not teach them to you. You can feel the effect of them, but that is all.'

One of the black belts went on with him. The Budokwai man did not make any throw; he just waited to see what the other man would do. The latter put up his right hand below his opponent's left elbow, and his left hand on top of the other elbow. Then he jerked his right hand up, and his left hand down. Nothing happened. He looked puzzled. He did the same thing again, and again nothing happened.

He look bewildered and said: 'I paid a hundred pounds for that trick. Every time I did that to my teacher, he was thrown through the air!'

'Did you ever try it on anyone else?' asked the secretary.

'No,' he said. 'I have never been attacked. I was absolutely confident that I knew it, and it would work.'

In this way, a number of people were swindled out of their money.

Mr. Tani and Mr. Koizumi were determined that the judo movement should have a good technical foundation. The standard was kept high – the first Dan would correspond to a second Dan in Japan. After two years, I was first *kyu* and took the examination for first Dan, the coveted black belt. There was one other candidate: he was smaller and lighter than I, but fairly skilful. I was big and strong and rather fast for a big man; I had some skill, but got most of my results by rushing the opponent. In the contests, we both did well against other first *kyu* grades. Then we had a one against six line-up. Both of us succeeded. Then we faced each other in a two-point contest; he made a mistake and was thrown with a big counter.

Now Koizumi and Tani briefly whispered together. They called out a second Dan, one of the strongest men in The Budokwai. One–point contest. I was still pouring sweat from the previous ones, but I felt I had nothing to lose, and charged at him. He was not warmed up, and did not react quickly enough. I smashed him with a big *harai-goshi*. I went home that night very satisfied with myself.

The list of promotions was posted up the next day. To my amazement, my name was not on it. But the first *kyu* whom I had defeated was promoted to first Dan. At first I thought it was simply a mistake, but the secretary told me that this was a correct copy of the list he had received from the two judges.

I was furious. I went down to the changing room, rolled up my *judogi*, towel and slippers, tied them with my humiliating brown belt and left the *dojo*. I resolved I would never go back. That week-end, however, a judo friend of mine called to see me. I did not say a word about judo. I was still simmering with anger and disappointment. Just before leaving he said, rather nervously: ' I overheard Mr Tani talking to Mr Koizumi yesterday. He was saying that even very good results, if they are got mainly by strength and speed, do not qualify for a black belt.'

I thought about this during the weekend and, on Monday, I turned up again at the *dojo*, and began practising, rather sulkily. Neither of the teachers, nor anyone else, said anything. At the next grading contests, I received the black belt. I thought how lucky it had been that my friend happened to overhear the bit of conversation between the teachers. Without that chance I might have given up judo. It was only later that I came to see how strange it was that these two Japanese should have been talking to each other in English.

So I believe that the teacher has two roles; one is technical, and the other is to do inner training. Perhaps one could also say that there are different kinds of teacher: one kind can teach only the technical side, another can teach the technical and the inner side, and there may be even some who can teach the inner side but not that particular technique.

The teacher of technique alone will become out of date in some things, unless he keeps revising his knowledge and practice. But the teacher of inner training will not become out of date, because he is not putting something new into the pupil. He is training something which is already in the pupil.

For example: a teacher of judo in Taisho times taught *uchimata* (inner thigh throw) as an *ashiwaza* or ankle technique: now it is a *koshiwaza* (hip technique). Then again, *tai-otoshi* (body drop) in Meiji times was done with the sole of the extended leg flat on the ground. This led to many injuries to the knee, which faced upward. So the throw was modified; today the extended leg rests on the toes, and the knee is turned to the side. These are improvements in technique. They are more scientific though the old methods could still be effective.

The inner training is quite different, and science has little to say about it. As an example, take the case of a young second Dan who has a strong right *osoto-gari* (major outer reap). His own natural inclination is to develop this more and more strongly. The others in the *dojo* will get to know it and will defend. But if it becomes very strong, they will have to exaggerate their defences. Suppose one of them defends by taking the leg back in anticipation of the coming *osoto-gari*. As it gets stronger, it will work even against a rear leg. Then the defender will have to take it back even further. Finally, he can certainly resist the *osoto-gari* but he will be very weak against even a weak *seoi-nage* (shoulder throw). This judo ends up as 'bull judo'. It has one very strong central technique, corresponding to the bull's horns. Around this, there are a few rather weak *waza*, which nevertheless can succeed against the unnatural positions of the defenders. These other techniques correspond to kicks by the bull. He is not very good at kicking, but they have some effect on a weakened opponent.

This 'bull judo', though it may be effective on the *tatami*, is very little help in life. It corresponds to skill at tennis, where the technique consists in controlling strength and direction of the shot. After playing tennis for six months, and occasionally attending first-class matches, one has seen everything that there is in tennis. Tennis gives a general fitness, though often rather one-sided, and precision in handling a tennis racket. Outside that, it gives nothing. The same thing goes for the *ippon-yari*.

Tricks

An experienced judo teacher can show a keen pupil one or two tricks which, if practised intensively, will get dramatic results in the first year. I remember a pair of friends who began judo at the same time, and worked together in a club in the country. In build they were thin and wiry, and also intelligent. They learnt from somewhere (not from me) two or three such tricks, and practised them more or less in secret, only with each other and a friend or two. They never used them in general practise.

When they came up to The Budokwai in London, the central club for grading, they would execute one of these tricks, and win sometimes in four or five seconds. The opponent, completely taken by surprise, would go over – bang! It was like a magician's trick, and they gained a fearsome reputation. It was also pleasant for the examiners, a break from the plodding monotony of so many beginners' contests. In a few months they had progressed to first *kyu* grade, and it was expected that they would go on in the same way. But now there was a change. They were meeting other first *kyu* grades, and first *kyu* grades have seen a good deal of judo. They could no longer surprise their opponents. And these tricks, like tricks in all fields of life, have no sound basis when the concealment has gone. A street trader's trick works only once.

These two found that they had no strong attack apart from the tricks, which now did not work in their contests. Their 'tricky' judo showed its limitations. The result was that they stuck at first *kyu* grade for over a year, while some of those whom they had beaten so brilliantly earlier on, now gradually overtook them and got a black belt before them. They could make no progress till they learnt some sound techniques.

There is a wider application. Success, especially dramatic success, is often in fact a set-back. With most of us, it means that we think: 'Oh, I am really good now.' In extreme cases, the successful man begins to think that he has a message for the judo world. The self-satisfaction can mean the end of his judo career. He does not advance further, though he may remain a formidable opponent at his own level.

But when you have a failure, you have to analyse, and realise: 'I am not good enough.' Then you make progress. In general, success blunts the edge of one's judo, whereas failure sharpens it. There are exceptions, I admit, but that is the general rule. This is why it is best to try to practise as much as possible against superior opponents, and not much against weaker opponents. With the latter, one can throw them even if the throw is not done well; it can easily lead to sloppy technique.

I used to watch Kyuzo Mifune practising with the small children at the Kodokan. He could have picked up the opponent with one hand and just laid him on his back. But in fact Mifune always made the few gentle throws he allowed himself, throws in perfect form. In this case, of course, it was not for his own sake, but to give the little boy a demonstration of that perfect form. The boy would not observe it consciously, but it would be taken in by him just the same as a feeling for the throw.

I myself used to watch him for another reason. I was taller than most of my opponents in Japan. In the 1930s, the difference between me and them was roughly the difference between Mifune (a small man), and some of the children. So I was learning how to handle opponents who were much shorter. They were of course very much stronger than Mifune's children, but there again Mifune used almost no force in making his throws there. The delicacy of his throws was, incidentally, most attractive to see and it gave me an insight into the beauty of real judo.

Kyuzo Mifune as a young fifth Dan

Manners

Among the judo fraternity in Japan, the roughest are the medical students. I practised once with such a man though at first I didn't know where he came from.

Now, normally in the *dojo*, people just come up and say '*O-negai*', ('Will you?'). But this chap came up and made a deep formal bow.

'*O-negai-itashimasu*'. ('May I have the honour of practising with you?').

'Oh, all right,' I replied.

When we started he was like a typhoon – all elbows and knees and hacks. Then he first threw me, and as I was getting off the floor, he drew himself up and said 'Please excuse me.' I thought, 'Whew, what is this?'

Then, when I threw him, the same thing happened. He got up off the floor, stood straight and said, 'Thank you very much.' And then it was all elbows, knees and hacks again.

I realised later that the teacher in the medical judo *dojo* knew that this formal manner was just what they needed. He insisted on very strict politeness so that it would calm them down, restrain them a little bit, just for a moment, in the middle of all the excitement. It would restrain them and hold them to something formal and peaceful, honouring and respecting the opponent. He knew how easily they could lose their tempers, so this restraint of manners allowed them to practise in other *dojos* without things getting out of hand.

The killer instinct, the temper, the fury

It does get results, but there is something higher. One of the analogies that is given is the yacht. Many people think that the yacht can go fastest when the wind is directly behind, blowing forward. But the yacht can go faster if it is across the wind. The mechanical principle involved is different – the inclined plane – and the yacht can go faster than the wind. Most people find this incredible, but it can be looked up and verified. (There has to be a keel to hold the boat steady.)

This example is given in Zen. The passions are not directly opposed, but they are crossed and so made use of in a spiritual way. The heart doesn't run directly before the passions. It runs across them.

A lovely style

It is vital in the application of the spiritual principles, as in judo techniques, that they must work. One hundred years ago, Zen master Iida made quite a point of this. He said things may be very beautiful; things may be very appealing; things may be very touching, very kindly. But unless they work, they're not Zen.

And in judo I can remember a beautiful stylist. He said to me once, 'You know, as I pick myself off the floor, they say, "Oh but you've got such a lovely style." '

Cutting off the bull's horns

In judo, when the teacher tells us (and he says this only to people who are determined to improve), 'You've mastered that technique. Now give it up for six months,' we think, 'What? I'm not allowed to do that? I go on the mat and I'm not allowed to do my big throw? I've got to try and do other things that I can't do? I'll get countered, I'll look an absolute fool!'

Now many of us fail this test. We think, 'Oh no! I'm not going to do this.' And we go back to what we can do, and we get some success.

But those who have faith in the teacher and who realise the teacher has got faith in them, follow his advice and give up their favourite technique for a while. They begin to develop a free movement, not fixed on one point. They can move freely. If the opportunity is there they can take it because their minds are not fixed on one throw or one situation.

We go round looking for opportunities, trying to create opportunities, so we can bring out the big gun. But actually people somehow get an instinct for not getting in front of a big gun, even though it may be hidden in the bushes.

These methods fail in the end, so we give them up. In judo it's called 'cutting off the bull's horns.' After eight years' intense practice, you develop something very strong and that's the bull's horns – that's what you fight with. Suddenly, you are asked to cut them off. And that means one becomes a beginner again.

This is a very important side of the spiritual as well as the technical side of judo training. The teachers also tell us, and they've put it into practice too, that when we're becoming strong and well-known, and we've mastered something, then we should take up something else where we are going to be no good at all. If you're a violinist, and you've mastered the violin, then take up the piano and you'll be stumbling over five-finger exercises. They say that when you've become a great big frog in your own pond and you're puffing your self up, go to the neighbouring pond and become a tadpole, a tiny little tadpole.

This is again 'cutting off the bull's horns' and being able to go freely into other forms.

Tigers and rabbits

In our western sports, and in a good many other things too, the tigers won't play with the rabbits. But in *budo*, however much of a tiger a man is – he's in the club team, perhaps in the county team, perhaps in the national team, and practises like mad – he always gives twenty minutes of his time every day to give instruction to a beginner, to a complete beginner, in order to help develop this unity. The purpose of *budo* is not that some are performing stars and the others are just watching them, but that there's a unity.

Specialities

We teach techniques which people can acquire. After perhaps eight years a man who's very keen and has a good teacher, can get an extraordinary skill in one or two moves. He then identifies himself with that skill he's got, and when he comes up to a contest he thinks, 'This is how I'm going to win – by this special technique I've developed.'

Of course, the first aim is usually to find out what special technique the other man has developed so that one can guard against it. Well, you generally get confusing and conflicting reports about a prospective opponent. Some people tell you 'Oh he goes off like a bomb at the beginning, but if you can survive that, he's got nothing. He's just got one terrific throw.' And then somebody says 'Oh no. He's given that up altogether! He hangs on now until the fourth minute, then he explodes.'

After you've had a certain amount of experience, you wipe all that aside and conclude, 'I'll just fight the man as he is.'

But for ourselves, we develop a speciality and we think we'll fight with that. We feel we can win with that. However, there's a limit to it. The speciality is something that is, so-to-speak, like a block of ice. It can't go through a sieve. As the standard goes up and the opponents are able to defend against our favourite techniques, we know we have to throw away that reliance on those special techniques and take the small and tiny opportunities as they occur. It's very difficult to do this, just as it's very difficult to give up one's particular technique which one's good at for handling life.

People come to the judo hall and they say 'Oh, I'm not very good at judo, but I am good at accounts and organising. I'll take over all the accounts and organising – do it for nothing. You'll all be free to practise.' Well, that's a very bad thing for a *dojo*.

Another man, he's a skilled carpenter; he's terrified of judo but wants to be associated with it, so he says, 'I'll do all the repairs.' And you have new benches and you have new racks and the *dojo* is transformed. But the members are doing nothing towards it, and that's very bad.

And you get another man. He'll clean out the showers and the lavatory and do it beautifully; they are spotless, but he's not doing much practice. That's bad for him and it's bad for judo enthusiasts. So in judo clubs we should try to prevent this happening. The team members, however good and skilful they may be, should take their turn to go on their knees scrubbing out the showers along with the others. This makes a difference to the whole atmosphere of the place; it brings a unity into it.

Predicting the result

Meeting a superior in grade
the only way to go is completely to forget
that the superior grade is bound to win.

This is a poem from the School of the Spear from the 14th or 15th century. The School of the Spear specially developed the psychological side because the technique of the spear is very simple. There is very little technical excellence – it's mainly instantaneous response and anticipation, so that there is no gap between the opponent's move and the response.

Then, as today, they used to be arranged in grades, which were regarded as important. If you were, say, a third Dan, and you were going to meet a fourth Dan, the expectancy was that you would lose.

The immediate reaction is, 'How can you forget that?' But it can be forgotten. The opponent may be a higher grade but that's all in the past and there's a lot of luck attached to attaining grades and a lot of luck attached to skills. The man may be having an off day.

The thing is completely to forget all that and to think 'Now!'

You have to think of the present moment, with no grades and no other circumstances of any kind.

Similarly, if the higher grade thinks, 'I'm bound to win', that is the way he'll lose, because he's not fully alert.

It is much easier for an expert to go on with somebody who has done judo for a year than it is with somebody who has never done it at all. If you go on against somebody who has done it for a year you'll know what he'll do; he'll do the 'right' things but he won't be good enough at them.

But with somebody who's never done it at all you've no idea what he'll do. Most of it will be absolutely useless, of course, but it will be unexpected.

There's a story in the East about the merchant who gets drunk and walks on top of a high wall. He falls off the wall, about thirty foot to the ground and he happens to fall on another merchant and, by extraordinary chance, kills him though he himself is unharmed.

So the magistrate says, 'Well, it was a kind of an accident but you did get drunk, so you have got to pay compensation to the sons.' So the merchant says, 'Yes, yes, of course.'

But the sons disagree strongly. They say, 'The law stipulates, a life for a life. In addition to the compensation this man should give his life; he's killed our father and his life should be forfeit.'

The magistrate explains that this age-old law is meant for cases of murder. But the sons insist, 'No! A life for a life. Justice!'

The magistrate says, 'Don't you think mercy might be better?'

'No,' they reply. 'Justice. We are asking for justice.'

The magistrate retorts, 'Well then, you'll have exact justice. My officers will put a rope around the merchant and stand him in the same spot where your father died. The two of you go to the top of the wall. First of all, the elder of you can jump, and if he misses, the younger can jump.'

In the same way, when you are up against an absolute beginner he'll do things so risky and crazy that you can find your hands full. He's jumping on you from the top of a wall. So he's much harder to handle than somebody who knows the rules and the ropes but isn't too good at them. He is much easier.

So, it is best to forget the circumstances of grade and 'Oh, he's bound to win/ he's bound to lose.'

These are the things which fix the result already which need not be fixed at all.

The new black belt

When a student of judo gets a black belt for the first time he becomes a kind of honorary teacher – in theory. In reality, he doesn't know much, but he has had to practise quite hard to get it. And when you get your first new black belt it's the greatest thrill in judo. You can go on to become a senior teacher after that and have various awards, but that's nothing to the thrill of your first black belt.

It's a new belt and it's very stiff so it's constantly coming undone because the knot is so stiff that it won't knot easily. And then you have to re–knot it and you look down and you see the black and it's all very satisfactory.

But what tends to happen is that as you are now expected to be rather good you have a certain authority in the hall. If there's nobody else there except beginners the danger is that you turn into a bit of a bully. Not that you are trying to hurt people – you just want them to be aware that you can throw them; and so you keep throwing them. After all, you think to yourself – if I do not constantly throw these weaker players, they may think I am going off! So you put another one in, and then another one just to make sure.

Of course, this has to be stopped, so we had a system for a new black belt. A few days afterwards, when he's in the *dojo*, the senior instructor has a word with some of the very experienced senior men and one of them goes across to the new black belt and asks for a practise. And they practise.

Well, the senior men who are considerably stronger never put in a really hard throw against that level, but this time they do. The new black belt is absolutely flattened, and then held on the ground; and then a strangle comes on and he feels he's going unconscious and he taps in surrender and the senior man says, 'No, you are not dead yet, go on struggling.' And the new black belt goes on struggling. The senior grade then lets off the strangle for a little bit – and on it comes again.

The new black belt is having a terrible time. He's pouring with sweat. Then the senior grade finally says, 'Right.' And they bow and off he goes.

Then the new black belt is leaning against the wall, trying to recover, and another senior grade comes up and does the same thing. Well, when the third one comes up, it's usual for the young chap to get a bit frightened, because they're really doing it hard and all sorts of thoughts start coming into his head. He starts thinking, 'They know I am going to be good so they don't want me up among their company. That's why they are trying to knock me out and injure me – so I'll never come again.'

All sorts of little thoughts go through his mind, and it's very easy to panic. He looks around the *dojo* and everybody is practising vigorously; and this young chap feels (and I've felt it and done it) himself getting a bit frightened but you can't leave the mat. You are even more frightened of doing that. The whole *dojo* is moving, practising, and then you notice something not moving. Through all the whirl and activity in the *dojo*, you see, across the mat, the old teacher standing there, watching. And that transforms the whole thing.

You now know that this is taking place under his gaze. He is aware of it, he's permitting it and it's for your good. The whole situation is transformed by just becoming aware that you are under that gaze. And somehow you survive and you become a fully-fledged black belt and you are no longer inclined to bully anyone.

Inspiration

You may think that everything that can be discovered has been discovered but that is not true.

In the old *jujitsu* schools which emerged during the prosperous times in Japan from the middle of the 16th century they used to hold inside the sleeve. You can get a very strong grip there and it is difficult for the opponent to break the grip.

After a hundred years somebody discovered that if, very rapidly, you put your hand around his you can break that thumb. It took a hundred years for that to be developed, but it was somebody's inspiration. Now it is a technique.

The old days were rough, but now, of course, there's a rule against breaking fingers in this way.

About fifteen years ago in Japan before a contest, a man went up to a referee and said, 'I believe this is now forbidden – you mustn't put any fingers inside the sleeve?'

The referee replied carefully, 'You must not hold the inside of the sleeve. You must hold the outside of the sleeve.'

But the man continued, ' Sir, I'm a plain simple man.' (Well, the referee should have known that when people say this sort of thing they are generally up to something!) 'What is the outside of the sleeve which I'm permitted to hold.'

The referee pointed to the outside of the end of the sleeve.

'Ah,' said the man. 'So if I hold *there* I'm alright. I'm keeping to the rules?'

'Yes,' retorted the referee.

Well now, what he did was to put his thumb on the outside edge of the sleeve, and then fold the outside of the sleeve inside. The referee was a bit caught.

So now they've changed the rules again. Instead of saying 'Don't hold inside' they say 'Don't hold inside the mouth of the sleeve'.

I give this example because the field is endless. One can think that everything has been researched and analysed by keen people but it isn't so.

And it's the same in our lives. There are many things about which we think, 'Oh I know that there's nothing new to come out of that.' But it isn't so.

Kangeiko

Going straight at a thing is a very important part of the training of the 'Ways'. One aspect of this is to practise under unfavourable conditions deliberately.

Suppose you're a poet – one day in the middle of winter you should get up at half past three, throw open the windows and, without any heating, write some poetry. If you are an archer, do the same thing. If you are a painter do the same, although your hand is blue with cold.

Cold training in judo used to be at about quarter to five in the midwinter, and it went on for a month. Well, it is very cold but it teaches you one thing. If you are very cold your body will only be sixty per-cent efficient, but you can make it sixty per-cent efficient. It is very, very cold. The windows are thrown open, it's five in the morning and your body is very cold – frozen.

You have to practise judo, but there are many things you can't do. You keep missing the timing and you stub your toes.

But if you can keep your awareness and calm and know that your body is only sixty per-cent efficient but you use that sixty per-cent to the full, that's a great advantage in life later on.

People who haven't been through that training are not efficient at all. They have no ability when the conditions are not right. They say, 'Oh, what can you do in cold like this?' They collapse completely.

But if you have done that training you can do something. And the same applies when you are ill or injured.

Disadvantages

A seventeen-year-old judo student who was very promising lost his right arm in an accident. When he recovered he began to go to the judo training hall again, and practised with the loose sleeve tucked into his belt. He could not throw anyone except a few friends who let him do so; when he told them to try hard his defences were completely broken and he could not get near to a throw himself.

His parents consulted with the judo teacher, and they made attempts to interest him in something else. 'You have a fine judo spirit,' the teacher told him, 'and now you can use that spirit to excel in something where you don't need two arms. You might try table tennis – show them what the judo spirit can do in that.' But his interest could not be diverted from judo. This sometimes happens – for a time a particular thing becomes the whole world, and it was so in this case.

When the boy realised that he would not be able to make up for his lost arm no matter how much he practised, he fell into a deep depression. He became unable to study, and hardly spoke. The parents again consulted the judo teacher who told them, 'I have no idea what to do. But we can take him to see my old master who is a spiritually advanced man. He lives in retirement and is a good way from here, but if I write to him I'm sure he will see us.'

So the four of them went to the old master, who had been contest champion in his time. He listened carefully, and asked the parent a question. 'Is it your intention that he should go to university?'

'Yes,' they replied, 'but he's not studying now.'

The master was silent for a little. He turned to the judo teacher: 'What is the standard of the students' championship in your county –

what grade are the finalists?'

'Well, as you know we are a small county, but the judo isn't too bad. The champion is generally not more than second Dan, but not under that either.'

The old master said to the boy, 'I can see that you will have to fulfil your ambition at judo before you can go on to anything else. Now to become student champion in your county in three years time – would that satisfy you?'

The young *judoka* could only gulp in bewildered acquiescence.

'Then you must undertake to study again, because if you don't study you won't be able to become student champion, will you? And I will make arrangements for your training, which you will have to follow without any question or doubts. It will be a rather hard time.'

When the parents had finished making their thanks, they departed with their son, leaving the younger judo teacher behind them. 'I suppose you think that I have been promising him something impossible in the hope that before the three years are over he will have become interested in something else?' said the old master. 'It could happen with some of them, but not that one. He will have to do it or die.'

'But master, how can he do it with the odds against him like that?'

'His disadvantage must be turned into an advantage. You remember how you used to have a bad habit of occasionally taking a wide step with your right foot? We reduced it by paying attention, but still occasionally you did it when there was a flurry. When I realised it would always be with you and would come out from time to time, I made you practise *hiza-guruma* (knee wheel) every day as a part of your routine. Perhaps you thought I was being eccentric, or giving you something unsuitable as a test of your will power? After all, you must have thought to yourself that *hiza-guruma* wasn't suitable to your build.

'But it has been quite useful to you in contest, hasn't it ? When you accidentally made that wide step, your opponent often automatically made a *kouchi* (inner reap) attack, and then your *hiza-guruma* was already sharpened for the counter. So your disadvantage, your tendency to make a wide step, became your advantage; they used to walk into an unexpected counter.

'You have the principle from your own experience, but it's not enough to know about it. You must find some way of applying it to the present case. It will be good for you to train this boy, because the experience will turn you into a real teacher of the Way and not just technique. Now think how you are going to turn his disadvantage into an advantage. Come back next week.'

When the teacher appeared again he blurted out, 'I've thought and thought about it. All I can see is that this boy has only one arm, and however hard he trains there will always be others with both arms who train just as hard. You know some of them are just as keen as he is. I can't see how he can ever do more than put up a gallant losing struggle.'

The old master said, 'In your ordinary classes train him in defence only. Even with one arm only he can get fairly expert at that – anyway, good enough to survive any rush attack at the beginning of a contest. Tell the other boys that it is a good opportunity to try their attacks against someone specialising in defence. He'll take some hammerings but that doesn't matter.

'Then have him in private at your *dojo* every morning for half an hour. Teach him a few *jujitsu* wrist turns which a man can do with one hand, and let everyone know that, so that they don't get inquisitive. They'll think that you're feeling sorry for him, and giving him some special training in something he can do with one arm. And that will be true. But the main part of the time teach him some variations on *hane-makikomi* and a special form of *osoto-makikomi*, which we can look at now.'

There are several forms of throw which are extremely effective if the thrower can get in properly, but which are easy to stop. The defender just has to press down with his hand on the attacker's arm, a small movement which can be made very quickly. To succeed, an attacker must make the complete movement with his whole body, covering the distance of perhaps two foot or more before the defender can make this small movement with the hand.

Judo men of any experience have a built-in reflex action of the hand against this whole case of throws, and it is not worthwhile spending several years mastering one of them when it can be so easily stopped. *Hane-makikomi* is one of the rare forms of this class of throw, and it is hardly ever seen.

The one-armed judo student kept up this training on these lines for three years. He had a sad time of pure defence in regular classes, and had to work very hard in the mornings with the teacher alone, practising the movements until they were as natural to him as breathing. He was told never to attempt them in public. As he got more expert, he often longed to score a few surprise successes against his regular opponents, but he managed to hold himself in. He put up with their pity and sometimes ridicule.

After three years he was entered for the students' championship, to the puzzlement of his fellow *judoka*. In the event he went straight through to become champion, winning in each contest in the first few seconds with *hane-makikomi* or *osoto-makikomi*. His opponents in the later rounds saw the technique, of course, but found they were unable to check it in time.

What happened was that when he came in, very fast, the reflex defensive hand action automatically functioned. But in this case there was no arm to press. This was a *judoka* with no right arm. The whole system of defence reflexes became confused at the unfamiliar feeling, and the throw came off. Theoretically a defender could make some other defence, but at these high speeds no ordinary *judoka* is able to modify his reflexes at short notice.

This is a striking example of the principle of turning a disadvantage into an advantage.

Arhat Pindala, Japan, 13th century.

The learning process

What you as a pupil think is a great success your teacher often has no enthusiasm at all for. And what you think is a terrible failure may sometimes please your teacher.

Now from the teacher's side I've often seen this. The chap's come up and he's got something that works. So he starts exploiting that and he doesn't make any further progress. But that's not what you want as a teacher. You don't want him showing off what he can do. You want him developing something more difficult where he's going to fail and look a fool.

But he doesn't want that.

So from a teacher's point of view those successes are nothing – they are a positive hindrance. Sometimes, when a pupil loyally tries something very difficult, he find himself being smashed with the counters and made to look an absolute idiot.

Some of these throws have got to be a hundred per-cent; you fail if you can only manage ten per-cent, you fail when you can only manage sixty per-cent, you fail when you only manage ninety per-cent. Well, the pupil can't see that. All he knows is, 'There I go, flat on my back again.'

But the teacher sees it. Speaking as someone who has taught, it's very difficult to convey that to pupils...extremely difficult.

Perhaps this may help you as pupils.

Surprise

As a young fourth Dan in Japan, I had a two-part contest, as an experiment, against a *kendo* man of the same grade. He knew almost nothing of judo, or I of *kendo*. The first contest was a judo contest. Beginners generally come forward in tiny steps, teeth clenched and arms outstretched stiffly; one just picks them off at leisure.

This man gave a yell and launched himself straight at my knees like a torpedo, in a sort of flying tackle. I was so surprised that I could not get out of the way, though I managed to double up as we went down so that I finished up on top and at once tied him up, partially saving face.

When it came to the *kendo* contest I knew it would be useless trying to imitate kendo technique. As we came to meet each other, I slid my right hand to hold the tip of the sword handle and jumped in the air, holding my wrist high and swinging the bamboo sword downward in a one-handed blow to his head.

A skilled *kendo* man protects his head by only just as much as is necessary and he made a defence to this unusual attack. But I was already much taller than most of his opponents, and the jump gave me extra height, so my bamboo sword did manage just to touch the top of his head. It would not have been a point by *kendo* contest standards, but it gave him a little surprise, like the one he had given me.

We both agreed we had learnt something from the experiment.

Falling

A drunken man falls from his carriage without hurting himself seriously, remarked Chuang-Tsu over two thousand years ago, because his body is relaxed and his spirit 'entire'. But actually confronting a fall, this knowledge is no use; the body automatically contracts and stiffens.

A judo student has to be trained to fall, to meet the ground all together instead of trying to keep off the ground and taking all the shock on one small point such as the wrist. After a time, he can meet a fall on the judo mat, and if the teacher says, 'Fall', he can do so.

Still, something is lacking. One day the teacher comes up behind him quietly and pulls him sharply over. If he falls then properly, it is 'part of him', he does it without knowing what he is doing. If the surprise makes him stiffen up, his training is incomplete.

Even after he can pass this test, there is one more. One day, he will fall over on ice or whatever it is, wholly by chance, and will fall properly. Once this has happened, it affects his walking and his judo practice, because before he had always been subconsciously afraid of falling. Now the ground is his friend.

The application in the Ways is to falls in life. To be able to take a disaster or a great failure with the whole personality, without shrinking back from it, like a big smack with which the judo man hits the ground. Then to rise at once.

Not to be appalled at a moral fall. Yet it is not that it does not matter. The judo man tries by every means not to be thrown, but when he is thrown it does not hurt him and in a sense it does not matter. It matters immensely, and yet it does not matter.

'Falling seven times, and getting up eight.'

Hane-goshi demonstrated with vigour and precision by T. Kawamura, a specialist in the technique which remains an example of judo at its most elegant although it is rarely seen in top competition nowadays.

Faith

I spent three years trying to master *hane-goshi* (spring hip) which I saw marvellously performed by a famous judo man, T. Kotani, when he visited London with Dr. Kano in 1935. My own teacher told me, 'You will never be able to use that as a contest technique; you had better stick to *harai-goshi*, which is similar but suits your build better. Your physique and movement is quite different from Mr Kotani's.'

But I was captivated by what I had seen, and in addition to the full training programme which my teacher set, I also practised about twenty minutes a day at *hane-goshi*. The teacher said no more, but after three years I had to admit he was right. I could only bring it off against much weaker opponents whom I could throw easily in any other way.

The teacher remarked, 'That was a good experience for you. Remember it when you come to teach. I did not say any more because *hane-goshi* is similar in many ways to *harai-goshi*, and I knew the practise you put in at it would help you with your own throw in the end.'

He referred to this incident once again much later on and said, 'At least you didn't complain that I had told you wrong. You tried for yourself and you found out. And you did keep up your practice with the things which I had told you to do. Some of them here try a throw for three weeks and then come to me and say, 'I've been trying it for three weeks now and still can't do it. Are you *sure* it is going to suit me?' I feel like saying to them, 'I myself have been trying it for thirty years now and still can't do it properly either!' I don't say it, but it has taken me a long time to get used to all these little doubts which Western people seem to have all the time.'

Later when I came to teach I realised the truth of his words. Sometimes after watching a beginner for some time carefully, I have concluded that his progress can be along such and such a path. I can see clearly in my mind's eye how his one-sidedness can change to a co-ordination of the whole body; how his shortness of arm can be turned to advantage by holding the tips of the opponent's sleeves. In my experience, I have seen each of these transformations several times, and been through similar ones myself. I estimate that he has enough interest in judo to keep up the practice.

But when I have told him what to do, after about three months I see a doubt coming up in his mind because he doesn't see much success and he seems to be getting worse. There is nothing more to tell him when he asks me about it. The seeds are there, and it is a question of watering them by practice, and waiting. When one is inexperienced as a teacher, one gets quite worried about the pupil's situation; his anxieties rub off on to the teacher, as it were.

But an older teacher realises it is useless to worry or even think about it. The thinking has been done already, and a proper programme has been carefully worked out to suit this pupil. Either he will follow it, or he will not.

Endurance

I began at judo under a Japanese teacher of the old school, practising every evening till the training period ended. One day I felt rather off colour, and prepared to leave early. The teacher said, 'Where are you going?'

I replied, 'I am not feeling very well: I will come tomorrow.'

He said, 'If a man comes up to you in the street with a hammer, wanting to kill you, can you say to him, "I am not feeling very well; come back tomorrow"?'

I remained that evening till he sent me home.

This one remark, heard only that time but never forgotten, was a big help later on when facing very gruelling training programmes.

Quick

I was once sitting on the edge of the mats, with some other spectators, watching some contests. It was not a big affair, and the little audience was mostly former students of the universities competing. I was there because I practised every day at one of them, and wanted to see how the team got on. We were in ordinary clothes, but without shoes.

One of the competitors tried to save himself from a throw by putting his arm out on to the mats as he went over. Of course, it is difficult to free an arm in time to do this, but in any case it is dangerous, and all judo men are warned not to do it. It can lead to a dislocation of the elbow joint. Still, in the rush of the contest, such warnings are often disregarded. In the present case, there was indeed an elbow dislocation. The lower arm stuck out at an unnatural angle.

The referee at once stopped the fight, but before he could do anything else, a middle-aged man shot out from the audience and sat beside the injured man, facing him. Very quickly he put one foot on the armpit, and the other on the side of the neck, and pulled the injured arm out straight. Then he lifted him to his feet, put his arm round his shoulders, and went out with him. I saw the boy's face as they went past; he did not seem in great pain, but more bewildered.

I made some inquiries afterwards, and learnt that the rescuer was a surgeon, and a fourth Dan judo man. My informant told me that experience showed that if an injury like that could be put right in a matter of a few seconds, there was very little inflammation afterwards, and healing was very rapid. If it could be treated within two hours, it could still be relatively quick. But after two hours, it might take a long time, and there could be permanent damage.

The same principle can be applied to the serious injuries of life.

Suppose we have a big disappointment; a message comes that something we had hoped for, and relied on getting, will not come to us after all. Suppose that someone we have helped now suddenly turns against us. These can be big shocks to our whole life. But as a matter of fact, they can be thrown aside fairly easily in the first few seconds.

The Chinese phrase is: 'Throw away the hundred troubles with one laugh.'

With that laugh, instantly, in the first few seconds, turn the attention vigorously to something that needs doing. Sweeping the garden, bringing order into a neglected pile of papers, clearing a cupboard, writing down proposals for the meeting. As soon as possible, immerse yourself in some longer constructive activity. If it cannot be done immediately, then within the two hours. If it has been practised, meditation on the navel-point of power will give independence. The anger or bitterness is felt only a little.

But if these things are not done, there is a rush of thoughts: 'How can people behave like this? I have lost my faith in human nature. Why do these things happen to me?' and so on and so on.

They can take a long time to heal, and there may be permanent damage which never heals.

Formal *zazen* (meditation) facing a rock garden in a Japanese temple.
Note the relaxed but firm posture.

Even effort

There has to be some effort in a judo technique, but Dr. Kano's principle was to make that effort efficient. In his time there were still some flourishing *jujitsu* schools (though not as flourishing as they had been). He studied their methods, and found that a good many techniques relied on surprise, together with extra strength developed by particular exercises. They were not using the body as an efficient unit. For this reason, they tried to keep their techniques secret. Although judo is no longer generally taught in this way, one sometimes sees something like it. If a man has a very strong right arm, he can get results with a poor technique because of the extra strength he has with that arm. Unless something is done to check it, he will develop more and more limited judo, and will not acquire a real mastery of it.

But it is not necessarily easy for a teacher to get him to change. One can explain to him that he must try to use the whole body as a unity, and if he is reasonable he will see and understand this. But when he actually tries to do it, the strong right arm takes over, and he gives s big punch with it in his usual way. He cannot stop the habit. He sees this himself, and says: 'What can I do? I just can't help it.'

In such cases I sometimes used an unusual method of training for a time. Suppose his big throw was *harai-goshi*, forced through with a punching action of the right hand. I knew that he had never actually felt his body acting as a unity; the consciousness of the strong right arm was always dominant, in spite of his efforts. So I used to put him on with a much weaker opponent. But I made him hold the jacket with only the little fingers of each hand.

'Now go ahead with your *harai-goshi*,' I told him. Of course if he had tried anything like his usual punch, he would have hurt his finger. So he was compelled to try to make a good *tsuri-komi*, taking the opponent onto his toes and then make the actual throw with a sweep instead of a punch. After surprisingly little experience, some students get the idea. It improves not only their *harai-goshi*, but their judo in general. For the first time they really understand what Dr. Kano meant.

We can try applying this principle in life. An injury to the right hand which prevents writing can be made an advantage. Serious attempts should be made to write with the left hand, instead of avoiding writing as much as possible during the healing period. With many of us, the body consciousness is poor in the inferior side, and this is a chance to develop it.

It is a principle of *budo* that the first field of study should ideally be judo, in which there is no weapon. The whole body is trained to get equal facility in all different movements on both sides. When this general facility has been acquired, the special techniques of fighting with weapons can be studied better. There's an old saying that if a student spends his first year studying judo, and then specialises in, say, *kendo* or the spear for five years, he will often be better at the special art than one who has done nothing but the special art from the beginning. I know that *kendo* men will say this is just the prejudice of a judo man, but I think there is some truth in it.

It comes down to the question: why do we do judo? The narrow answer is: to win contests. The true answer is: to train body and mind to act efficiently in life.

Exceptional ability with a right-hand punching action could give a winning advantage for a time in judo contests, but it does not train the whole body. So it gives nothing for life in general. Other methods of trying to win a contest, such as making insulting remarks at the opponent, taking drugs, even trying to bribe the referee, might in some cases help to win a contest. But again, they offer nothing for life itself.

One who trains at judo in the proper way gets a big advantage in life: he can quickly learn to drive a car or handle a computer, he can easily pick up skills like golf or tennis or do-it-yourself jobs. Then he has the courage to face, when necessary, being laughed at – for instance when he makes mistakes learning a foreign language.

Judo men are used to falling. They jump up at once, and are not at all inwardly upset: they know it is part of the learning process. But the ordinary person hates falling: it is undignified, and possibly dangerous. Generally, they are ashamed of making a mistake, and sometimes they will simply not try anything where they may lose badly.

There is a saying, found in some form both in the East and the West: 'There is no certain way of winning at chess. But there is a certain way of not losing at chess: don't play chess.'

A strong desire to win at any cost, or fear of losing, represents a complete misunderstanding of sport. The interest of sport is the contest, within the rules; the satisfaction is in the struggle itself, and it is not important afterwards which side has won. A particular result is important at the time, and we try very hard for it, but it is not the real point of the game. Every sportsman knows that if he always wins, the game has no interest; the opponent is too weak to give a proper struggle.

Just as over-specialisation in judo can damage its use as a general training of the body-mind, so over-concentration on winning can damage sport as a training for life. Since money-making and political prestige have become important in sport, the desire is to win every time, by any methods. This is no longer sport, but at best a spectator entertainment, and at worst a sort of international warfare. It makes enemies, not friends.

One of the great purposes of sport is to make friends through a temporary make-believe struggle. Afterwards the competitors are no longer competitors; they congratulate each other on a good fight, which is yet not a fight.

Some historians believe that the reason why there was a blood-stained French revolution, but no such revolution in England, was because cricket was played so widely in England whereas the French landlords had to spend most of their time at the King's court at

Versailles, and so they were away from their estates. They did not know how their agents at home were oppressing the peasants.

The English gentry did not dance attendance at Court much; they stayed on their estates, and they played cricket with their tenants. After the game, they would drink ale together, and the local squire would hear, directly or indirectly, what was going on in the local villages. If things were bad, he would in many cases quietly try to improve them. The peasants did not have the same intolerable conditions as in France, and so there was no revolution and no guillotine.

Let me try to sum up. Both sport and *budo* were interesting and healthy pursuits, involving some sort of struggle and often rivalry. The purpose was not simply to achieve victory. Sport as it developed, especially in Britain, became a training in struggling hard but somehow remaining detached from success or failure: a good sportsman remained undisturbed in either case. He could accept the bad luck which everyone meets at times in sport with calm, or even a smile.

There was a vague ideal of applying this attitude even in situations of life and death. A good sportsman is not afraid to play dice with death. While he lives, he plays with life as a game. In his sport, he must have respect for his opponent; furthermore, a common interest in a particular sport leads to friendship.

Budo is a much deeper training. It directly trains for two things, which are only hinted at in the sportsman's training: freedom from the fear of death, and a certain freedom from anxiety as to what may happen.

The mania to win, and the degeneration into spectator sport, is contrary to the whole point of practise or *budo* or sport. There is a danger that they become a show, where a few stars, motivated by money or prestige, perform before masses of passive onlookers. Even the stars have very short careers; once past their peak, they sink into obscurity. In spite of momentary excitements, the general atmosphere is deadening. This is why hooligans riot at soccer matches: they do not themselves play any disciplined game, but they want some action. So they take to the undisciplined and destructive fighting of children. Sports stars may seem energetic, but in fact few of them can concentrate long on any one thing; it is all short-term excitement, almost useless for life.

If the ideal of sport, and still more the ideal of *budo,* is pursued, it strengthens will and endurance, and gives inner calm. It cannot be done if there is narrow focusing on just one part of the training; the training must be even and broad. To focus on only one technique will narrow the physical capacity; to focus on tricks will cramp the mental capacity; to focus just on winning will paralyse the spiritual capacity of calm and freedom.

But with proper practice, the whole personality is energised. He can see clearly in life, and face death. This was Dr. Kano's principle.

Hold

Hold tightly, let go lightly: this maxim for life is found in various forms all over the East. It can be exemplified in judo in a concrete form. Suppose my right hand (palm up) holds my opponent's left wrist.

He struggles a bit to make me instinctively hold tighter. Then he joins his hands, and walks round me in a quarter circle, on my right. This brings the force of his whole body movement in a lever action against the grip of my fingers, the fulcrum being my right hand.

As I continue to hold, I get a severe pain in the hand, and am drawn off balance. He easily frees his hand, leaving me hopelessly out of position. But if I can act consciously, and not instinctively, the result is quite different. As soon as I feel the leverage and realise that I cannot keep my hold, I instantly give it up. He continues the movement, but now there is not the expected resistance. So he tends to lose balance a bit. I can use my now free hand to give a little extra push, which unbalances him further; so now it is I who have the advantage.

(If he is a trained man, of course, he will cease his own movement when he feels my hold has gone. Then we both retain balance: we are well matched.)

The application to life is easy to see from this example. If I hold something tightly – money, reputation, someone's affection, a position of advantage, or even personal individual life itself – the course of events will one day irresistibly wrest it from me. When I realise that this is going to happen, I should not desperately try to hold on, but give it up at once, completely and without any lingering regret.

People say: 'How could it ever be done?' It can be done on the same basis as the judo example. When one grips something, the instinct is to grip harder and harder if the thing begins to be pulled away. Attention and purpose become focused on this small thing. I must keep it, I must keep it, I must prevent its going away. I instinctively restrict its freedom, by taking it as my possession. But as a matter of fact this restricts my own freedom also; I do not want to let it move away from me, but I also cannot move away from it. I cannot let it go, so I am equally imprisoned by it.

The point of judo is to retain freedom of movement; to hang on to the opponent's wrist is to be fixed there. Then as it moves, my balance is disturbed. The solution, in life as in judo. is to let it go and give a little final push at it.

We see this in all the truly free, in the West as in the East. When the audience was laughing at the mocking representation of Socrates on the stage in the play by Aristophanes, in the interval Socrates stood up from his seat and called out: 'And now here is the real thing to laugh at.'

In Japan, when the general Nobunaga was trapped in Honno-ji, he set fire to the ground floor so that no one could enter. Then he appeared on a balcony, and danced one of the solemn Noh dances, until the flames consumed him. His profession was life-and-death, and he showed freedom from both of them.

Most of us are not required to demonstrate it so dramatically, but the principle of 'hold tightly, let go lightly' can be applied at every level. If it can be done even partially, it will enlighten and invigorate everyday life, and perhaps give a glimpse of something beyond, hidden in the everyday.

The delicate image of Mirokubosatsu in Horyuji, Kyoto.